Stars are an integral part of the global film industry. This is as true today, in the age of celebrity culture, as in the studio era. Each book in this major new BFI series focuses on an international film star, tracing the development of their star persona, their career trajectory and their acting and performance style. Some also examine the cultural significance of a star's work, as well as their lasting influence and legacy. The series ranges across a wide historical and geographical spectrum, from silent to contemporary cinema and from Hollywood to Asian cinemas, and addresses both child and adult stardom.

SERIES EDITORS
Martin Shingler and Susan Smith

PUBLISHED TITLES
Elizabeth Taylor *Susan Smith*
Star Studies: A Critical Guide *Martin Shingler*

FORTHCOMING
Brigitte Bardot *Ginette Vincendeau*
Sabu *Michael Lawrence*

Nicole **KIDMAN**

PAM COOK

A BFI book published by Palgrave Macmillan

First published in 2012 by
PALGRAVE MACMILLAN

on behalf of the

BRITISH FILM INSTITUTE
21 Stephen Street, London W1T 1LN
www.bfi.org.uk

There's more to discover about film and television through the BFI. Our world-renowned archive,
cinemas, festivals, films, publications and learning resources are here to inspire you.

Palgrave Macmillan in the UK is an imprint of Macmillan Publishers Limited, registered
in England, company number 785998, of Houndmills, Basingstoke, Hampshire RG21 6XS.
Palgrave Macmillan in the US is a division of St Martin's Press LLC, 175 Fifth Avenue, New
York, NY 10010. Palgrave Macmillan is the global academic imprint of the above companies and
has companies and representatives throughout the world. Palgrave® and Macmillan® are
registered trademarks in the United States, the United Kingdom, Europe and other countries.

Designed by couch
Cover images: (front) *Nine* (Rob Marshall, 2009), © Guido Contini Films, LLC; (back) *The Hours* (Stephen
Daldry, 2002), © Miramax Film Corp./Paramount Pictures Corporation

Set by Cambrian Typesetters, Camberley, Surrey
Printed in China

This book is printed on paper suitable for recycling and made from fully managed and sustained
forest sources. Logging, pulping and manufacturing processes are expected to conform to the
environmental regulations of the country of origin.

British Library Cataloguing-in-Publication Data
A catalogue record for this book is available from the British Library
A catalog record for this book is available from the Library of Congress
10 9 8 7 6 5 4 3 2 1
21 20 19 18 17 16 15 14 13 12

ISBN 978–1–84457–488–9

CONTENTS

ACKNOWLEDGMENTS

Martin Shingler's enthusiasm was inspirational and his detailed comments on the manuscript invaluable. I'm also indebted to Rebecca Barden and Sophia Contento at BFI Publishing; project manager Chantal Latchford; staff at the BFI National Library; and archivist Judith Seef at the Australian Theatre for Young People (atyp).

Warm thanks for contributions and support to Twitter correspondents bookworm1979, bazthegreat, NicolesMagic and KINOWORDS; Ana Fernandez; Tim Bergfelder; and Sam Cook and Greg Ward.

INTRODUCTION

In recent years star study has evolved from semiotic, ideological and sociological analysis to take in the significance of stars in the history of Hollywood as a business, conceived as the centre of global media industries. In this light, the history of stardom from the early picture personalities to today's personal star brands emerges as one of increasing commodification. In investigating the phenomenon of star power scholars focus on stars' value in selling films (and themselves) as part of the market-driven enterprises of global media conglomerates, looking at their promotional activities and their function in branding processes. A related body of academic work explores the impact of celebrity culture on modern stardom. Alongside this scholarship, studies have developed that reconceptualise screen performance, paying detailed attention to the visual and sonic aspects of cinematic acting. Despite their differences, these approaches tend to view stars as the effects of a system, whether economic, social or representational, rather than as real individuals who act independently. By contrast, star discourse that circulates in the public media creates characters and storylines that depict stars as real people involved in personal and professional dramas, building recognisable identities for them. As many have pointed out, stars are contradictory entities that cross all these areas.[1] Depending on who is looking and from where, star images provoke conflicting responses, fantasies and desires. The challenge for star study is to unpick the intricate intertextual relationships between the different arenas in which star discourse appears, while research on individual stars is faced with the task of examining the shifting persona in all its manifestations.

With the explosion of electronic communication networks, this undertaking has become more difficult, as the recycling of star discourse is distributed across a proliferating number of sites. In this fluid situation the star persona is made and re-made in consumer interactions with media outpourings that are largely impervious to academic critique and are not easy to apprehend. Nicole Kidman exemplifies this quandary; she epitomises the modern commodity star whose image is dispersed across a bewildering array of media forms. As a product of the contemporary entertainment industries, she appears in film, theatre, television, music videos, commercials, press, live shows, magazines, books and online publications. The result is a fragmented persona that emerges as a collection of masks or images that do not cohere into an individual character, despite attempts to endow her with authenticity. In the following pages, I attempt to build a picture of the operations of Kidman's multifaceted star persona across different, related fields of activity, avoiding the temptation to view them as entirely circumscribed by commercial interests but without denying her commodity status. My view is that commodities have symbolic and cultural significance as well as being profit-motivated and I am interested in the ways in which these aspects intersect to produce the Kidman star phenomenon.

My analysis is divided into three parts: in the first I offer an overview and a timeline, tracing the development of Kidman's career from its Australian beginnings to her ascension to international celebrity stardom. I look at the impact of her move to Hollywood on her transformation from tomboy into glamour icon and at the way her image and performance became characterised by pastiche. The influence of life events, such as her marriage to Tom Cruise, is assessed and I endeavour to evaluate Kidman's success in managing the ups and downs typical of contemporary stardom and celebrity culture. This chapter introduces the key areas and concepts explored in detail in the rest of the book. The second focuses on her film acting and her development of a distinctive style defined by 'actorliness', using recent scholarship on screen performance to illuminate her approach and the ways in which it has been received. I analyse her deployment of gesture and voice in a selection of titles that have been pivotal in her career, looking at the textual and extra-textual dimensions of performance. I contend that in the context of Kidman's global star identity, her stylised acting has postcolonial implications deriving from her Australian roots. Finally, I suggest that her emphasis on artifice and technique points to a conception of screen acting that looks to cinematic expression rather than to the actor's body and intentions for the realisation of character.

In the final chapter I explore the construction of her persona outside cinema in specific areas of the media and its dependence on performance of character types. The performance of celebrity has been neglected in favour of the star's acting in films; I attempt to redress the balance by demonstrating that celebrity appearances are governed by specific conventions and performance styles. In a series of case studies, Kidman's fragmented persona is shown to be portrayed and received differently according to context, although certain features recur. I look at attempts to provide a coherent identity by recourse to her Australian backstory and the ways in which core elements such as national identity, beauty, whiteness and feminism are mobilised. I propose that, through the construction of her persona, Kidman is projected as a heroic character in her journey to international success. As an example of modern star celebrity, her cultural significance can be measured as much by her willingness to engage with the demands of commodity stardom as by her achievements in film acting. Although each chapter deals with separate areas of stardom, the connections between the different spheres form a central part of my discussion. In this, I differ from approaches that treat aspects of star-making and star activity as independent entities.[2] In the context of the synergies characteristic of the contemporary global entertainment industries, I see performance as emerging from a dynamic relationship between interlinked media events.

Writing about Nicole Kidman increased my awareness of the potential for individual star analysis to open up diverse methods and areas of investigation. I have tried to adopt a multidimensional approach that embraces the various ways in which the star system can be conceptualised. Many of the topics covered here reach beyond the borders of screen studies to political, ethical and philosophical issues; within the limits of this project, it has only been possible to touch on those wider implications. My primary concern is to provide a better understanding of the operations of contemporary commodity stardom through close attention to the life and work of one of its most high-profile and successful exponents. As part of this undertaking I engage critically with some of the precepts that inform approaches to stars and star studies. As a result of structural, industrial, economic and technological changes, modern star-making diverges in many respects from the classic system and demands new analytical methods capable of getting to grips with its complexities. I attempt to show some of the directions in which such methods might develop.

1 STARDOM

A star is made many times over

In this chapter I explore the nature of Nicole Kidman's stardom and how it is made. Kidman is a prime example of a contemporary, global star phenomenon that is the product of industrial, economic and technological changes over the last twenty years. Her rise in the 1990s from Australian actress to international movie star has been related as a personal journey, characterised by emotional and professional peaks and troughs, that is as compelling as any film in which she has appeared. This endlessly enthralling story is told and retold via myriad media outlets dedicated to grabbing our attention in the maelstrom of today's celebrity culture. I want to look at the way Kidman's life story is used to manufacture her stardom, but also at how it can work to deconstruct and fragment her image. On one hand, the star biography can provide coherence in the face of the confusing mass of visual information, sounds and texts that mediate the star to the public; on the other, it is often perceived with scepticism as one of many unreliable sources, the result of publicity hype. This dichotomy, like many of the contradictions embodied by stars, feeds fantasies and anxieties about knowledge, power and control and can produce a wide variety of responses from adulation to scepticism.

     One of the most striking aspects of Nicole Kidman's stardom is the overwhelming proliferation of images, texts and media that

Nicole Kidman performs 'Somethin' Stupid' in Robbie Williams music video (Vaughan Arnell, 2001, EMI Chrysalis)

surround and create it. Films, television, theatre, press and magazine coverage, photographs, commercials, advertisements, music videos, promotional appearances, fan and official websites work together to sustain and manage a high degree of public visibility for the actress and her work. Through this kaleidoscope of clashing fragments, Nicole Kidman appears as multifaceted, contradictory and controversial: a powerful, financially successful figure in the global media industry; a philanthropist and outspoken defender of human rights; a leader of style and fashion; a feisty feminist; and a vulnerable human being. Online discussion boards debate her acting skills, her sexuality, the ageing process and its effects on her face and body, her assumed plastic surgery and intimate details of her private life. A vast array of international celebrity publications, from glossy lifestyle monthlies such as *Vogue*, *Vanity Fair* and *Harper's Bazaar* to tabloid gossip magazines, produces a flow of visual representations that promote, analyse and dissect the Nicole Kidman persona.

Star images are manufactured from these exchanges between connected elements of global media organisations. An industry of managers and press agents is devoted to controlling (not always successfully) the profligate amount of material that results. Stars actively contribute to the process by revealing or withholding information about themselves, by 'putting the record straight', by posing for photographs and by making celebrity appearances. Their activities in this sphere rely just as much on their acting training as do their performances in film, theatre and television, though they do not receive the same degree of critical attention. The manufacture of star images through publicity machines is perceived as belonging to the realms of commercial exploitation, in contrast to the film performance, which is the product of art and craft. Yet the intensification of promotional outlets and opportunities for consumer interaction in the post-internet era, together with the increased synergies between different media forms emerging from the reorganisation of global industries, have produced conditions in which it is more difficult to privilege one element over another. With the expansion in DVD, television and online access, the film itself, once the primary focus of critical analysis, has become one element in a matrix of interlocking discourses, each of which demands consideration. Studies of celebrity and fandom now engage with the commodification process, situating films in wider cultural and commercial networks. With this shift the focus of analysis extends beyond the boundaries of the film text to areas previously defined as subsidiary.[1]

Despite the widespread understanding of stardom as spanning multiple media sites and forms there is still a paucity of studies exploring the intersection of different operations and discourses. In *Heavenly Bodies*, Richard Dyer argues that star images are and always have been 'extensive, multimedia, intertextual' but that 'not all these manifestations are necessarily equal'. While admitting to paying more attention to film texts himself, he acknowledges that different aspects of a star's image, life and work can take precedence at different periods in their career and according to production and reception contexts.[2] The complexities of the image-construction system and its many agencies are almost impossible to grasp, let alone analyse – a difficulty that has mushroomed with the expansion of cross-media interaction. Dyer opens up the mechanics of star-making, which he traces across a series of structural oppositions.[3] Central to his argument is the notion that our fascination with the 'real' person behind the image is what draws us to stars and the public discourses through which we experience them. Consumers of star images search for the 'truth' of the person even though we are aware that we can only know them as image. It is this lack of access to the real person that partly motivates the fan to accumulate memorabilia, the detractor to debunk the star image and the critic to pore over media artefacts to decipher meaning. All these activities are designed to compensate for the fact that the star identity is fluid and elusive. We fabricate for ourselves, largely through fantasy, a coherent character or persona for the star from bits and pieces.

This can be seen as a creative process in which the images and texts offered by the star-making machines are re-ordered by consumers in their own interests. In the case of the critic or academic, a distance must be established between the profit motives of the star system and the perspective of the cultural analyst – a distance that is largely irrelevant to the fan. Critics and academics, of course, are also fans and fans can be critics, in so far as they do not always take the products of the star-making industry at face value. They all weave narratives and make judgments based on more or less sophisticated engagement with the materials at their disposal. All make sense out of the incoherent outpourings of the media. It is arguable that the perception we have of the star as a discrete, continuous, authentic human being derives as much from consumer activity as from industry-led image construction. Without denying that the industry trades on the idea that there is a 'real person' behind the star through biographies, production notes, interviews and so forth,[4] the renewed emphasis on branding and the scattering of information about the star across so many different sites seem to have made coherence and authenticity less achievable in the contemporary period. They may also be less desirable, as I shall suggest in relation to Nicole Kidman. Kidman's image is made up of multiple, contradictory representations both on and off screen. It has been argued that this chameleon quality enables her to play many different roles in life and art and makes her the quintessential contemporary 'commodity star'. The fact that she remains unknowable despite her ubiquity in myriad media forms is one of the reasons she fascinates us.[5]

Nicole Kidman embodies the ambivalences and contradictions of the contemporary media landscape, where image is everything and the search for veracity is doomed to failure. The 'real' Nicole Kidman is an effect of representation; we know that she exists, but our access to her is so highly mediated that she remains pure image, an icon. The dominance of images is a source of pleasure, as we admire and revere the star's beauty, but it is also a source of anxiety because images cannot be trusted. The ugliness lurking behind the star image is a major feature of celebrity journalism, where candid photographs claim to reveal the reality beneath glamorous appearances in yet another layer of representation. There is always a question mark over the contemporary star's identity, a doubt that compels us to delve beneath the surface, not to get to an absolute truth but to compile our own versions, which are never final.[6] It is this continuous process of playing with fickle images that characterises contemporary star-making. Stories about the star's life, which are equally unreliable whether they emanate from the horse's mouth or gossip magazines, play an important role in the construction of our shifting understanding of who the star is.

As Dyer and others have indicated, personal biography and the star name are essential to the construction of star identity.[7] The nomenclature 'Nicole Kidman' indicates that the star exists as an individual person despite the conflicting accounts of her. A personal history is made available via various sources that provides a backstory for a character we follow through a series of life events. The life history is reproduced many times in different locations; like myth and legend it is transformed in the retelling. 'Nicole Kidman' is as much a fiction as the roles she plays and though she is distinct from her film parts, she is forged in dialogue with them. In one of the few studies of visual images and modern stardom Jeannette Delamoir examines the stories created by Australian women's magazine coverage of Tom Cruise and Nicole Kidman's 2001 marriage break-up in the production of what she calls 'visual memory'.[8] She argues that, in the face of the deluge of images surrounding this major celebrity event, the circulation of photographs of the couple in magazine coverage provided an interpretive context for conflicting reports. This enabled 'a process by which visual memories [we]re unpicked and then knit together again into different formations'.[9]

Delamoir analyses the way older photographs of the Kidman–Cruise couple were recycled to make new configurations that told the tale of their relationship and its shock demise. Readers were offered the opportunity to relive and deal with the trauma through revisiting a huge number of carefully stage-managed pictures depicting happy coupledom, together with more intimate family shots. Some of the coverage returned to the rumours that circulated around the couple's relationship and their sexuality, implying that the gossip may have been true. In the absence of any hard knowledge or insider revelations, the retrospective look at what had happened facilitated a process of negotiation between different narratives in a search for the truth and the meaning of images. Both Kidman and Cruise's star personas were destabilised and stories were featured that presented their relationship as fractured and flawed.

Nicole Kidman's relationship with Tom Cruise continues to be a key element in her stardom even now when both she and Cruise have remarried.[10] The reasons for their break-up remain private and therefore a perpetual source of speculation and gossip. Delamoir's article reveals the importance of personal backstory in constructing the star persona but it is also a specific case study of the intersection of different discourses and conflicting narratives in producing the volatile entity that is contemporary celebrity stardom. Kidman's identity and her story are constantly in flux; as noted, this is part of her appeal, but it also works to alienate those members of the public

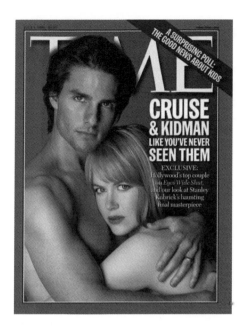

Celebrity couple: Tom Cruise and Nicole Kidman in 1999 (*Time* magazine, 5 July 1999)

who perceive her as false, or as hiding behind a mask. By reclaiming the meaning-making process from those who produce star images, consumers achieve a measure of control over those images and a sense of power over the star themselves. They may also feel closer to the person behind the image or that they know them personally, which may explain why stars are often referred to by their first name or a nickname. The central paradox of stardom – the tension between presence and absence identified by scholars – is said to culminate in the film performance, where the fragments produced by media hype cohere into the desired complete figure.[11] However, we may question whether this imaginary coherence is the primary focus of consumer desire in the context of modern celebrity stardom. The stories that circulate across diverse media outlets are equally powerful in encouraging us to participate in the star-making process itself.

The Nicole Kidman story

The task of researching this book brought the issues raised above into sharp focus. Compiling a reliable, complete Nicole Kidman biography from the mass of conflicting and unsubstantiated material devoted to the star proved impossible. Nicole Kidman herself was approached via various press agents but did not respond. In the face of this lack of hard evidence, my tactics in reconstructing the star became less driven by completion than by the negotiation of gaps and inconsistencies. The central character of the story faded in and out of focus as my attempts to give her substance in a linear narrative were frustrated. This is an interesting dilemma in the age of information technology when direct access to knowledge is increasingly assumed. Information about Nicole Kidman is characterised by varying degrees of inaccuracy, while knowledge of her is a scarce commodity. This is the case even though she appears to be frank and forthright in interviews. Her comments about her life and work, usually tied in to a film release or some other work or life event, are specific to context and time sensitive. And, of course, they are framed by journalistic and editorial choices. By a process of repetition, certain details are recycled until they become conventional wisdom whether they can be verified or not.

On this shifting terrain, there are key navigational aids: matters of public knowledge attached to the Nicole Kidman name that underpin the mutable persona. These provide the bare bones of a life story. Nicole Mary Kidman was born on 20 June 1967 in Honolulu, Hawaii to Australian parents, Antony and Janelle; both parents and her younger sister Antonia occasionally feature as characters in the star narrative. She has dual US–Australian citizenship and is a practising Catholic. In 1971, she moved with her family to Sydney, Australia, where she was educated. At this point, dates and events become blurred. Apparently a shy and isolated child, at the age of ten or eleven she became interested in acting and took weekend classes at Sydney's Phillip Street Theatre for around three years. She attended North Sydney Girls High School up to Year 11, where she met long-term friend and fellow actress Naomi Watts. In the early 1980s, she joined the Australian Theatre for Young People (atyp) in Sydney as a workshop participant; in 1984, aged seventeen, she appeared in two atyp productions: Frank Wedekind's *Spring Awakening* and *A Daniel Come to Judgement* by Allan Mackay.[12] During this period she was apparently auditioned by Jane Campion for her short film, *A Girl's Own Story* (1984), but was unable to take the role because of school commitments. This was an auspicious meeting and Kidman would later work with Campion on *The Portrait of a Lady* (1996) and *In the Cut* (2003).

There is no detailed information available about the teenage Nicole Kidman's acting training. The early 1980s were clearly productive years in which she acquired invaluable experience and industry contacts. In 1983, she left school and went to live in Melbourne for several months to work on the Disney television series *Five Mile Creek* (1985).[13] The same year she made her screen debut in the music video 'Bop Girl', in which Pat Wilson performed her smash hit.[14] Kidman had her first starring role as Helen in *Bush Christmas* (1983) and gave a feisty turn as Judy in the cult action-teen pic *BMX Bandits* (1983). Between 1983 and 1985, she appeared in several television productions and films and, as a result of her work on *Five Mile Creek*, was apparently approached to work in the US, although after a trip to Los Angeles she decided to stay in Australia.[15] In press and publicity coverage, a Nicole Kidman persona emerged of an independent, down-to-earth and strong-willed young woman with boundless energy and interests and ambitions beyond acting. Her striking appearance (abundant flaming red hair and pale skin) gained a lot of attention and in 1984, she was photographed by Patrick Lichfield for *Harper's Bazaar* in a feature on the ten most beautiful women in Australia.[16] Her physical beauty and intelligence were key factors in singling her out as an emerging star and she was sometimes compared to a young Katharine Hepburn. She was not afraid of controversy: she had a much-publicised relationship with co-star Tom Burlinson, eleven years her senior, which began while they were working on *Windrider* (1986), in which she had some brief nude scenes.[17]

The mid-1980s were decisive for Kidman's burgeoning stardom. A 1986 press interview demonstrated her keen understanding of her role in the star system as promoter of herself as well as her film and television work. She actively participated in building her persona as an actress and human being with strong opinions and an awareness of her sexuality. Although the material she appeared in was geared towards the youth market rather than critical acclaim, she projected herself as seeking more challenging and complex female roles.[18] Her media appearances demanded the performance of a personal, social and professional identity in interviews and photo shoots. This involved creating scenarios in which she portrayed herself as a character who was often similar to those she played in films and television. Many of the attributes of the Nicole Kidman persona constructed at this time, including pride in her Australian identity, have remained in place, with shifts in emphasis, over the years.

Several of the parts played by the teenage Kidman were tomboys: for example, Annie in *Five Mile Creek*,[19] Helen in *Bush Christmas*, Judy in *BMX Bandits* and Amy in *Watch the Shadows Dance* (1987). Others were rebels: Catherine in *Archer* (1985),[20] rock singer Jade in *Windrider* and athlete Carol in *Winners: Room to Move* (1985). Most of the productions featured distinctively Australian storylines in which her characters represented values of strength, courage and independence. The modernity of these female characters was encapsulated in her role as freethinking Megan Goddard in the acclaimed miniseries *Vietnam* (1987), for which she received an Australian Film Institute (AFI) award.[21] As she

An Australian tomboy: Nicole Kidman in *BMX Bandits*

embarked on a transition to adult roles, her looks and sexuality came to the fore (*Windrider; Emerald City*, 1988) but these portrayals were equally spirited. For the most part Kidman's acting style during her Australian years could be described as naturalistic, in the sense that her performance revealed the characters she played rather than drawing attention to herself as actress or star.[22] Even so, her aspirations to stardom were evident in the increasingly international scope of her projects (*Un' Australiana a Roma*, 1987; *Bangkok Hilton*, 1989; *Dead Calm*, 1989).

Dead Calm is perceived as the breakthrough title that propelled Nicole Kidman (and director Phillip Noyce) to Hollywood. It was produced by Kennedy Miller Productions – the team behind iconic Australian titles such as the *Mad Max* trilogy (1979–85) and *The Year My Voice Broke* (1987) as well as the *Vietnam* and *Bangkok Hilton* miniseries – with Hollywood major Warner Bros involved as US distributor.[23] It was clearly a tilt at the American market, featuring US actor Billy Zane as the psychotic killer Kidman's Rae

Ingram must defeat in order to save herself and her husband (Sam Neill). It now appears as a vehicle for Kidman, the culmination of her independent woman roles so far. In genre terms, *Dead Calm* crosses over between art cinema, thriller, action movie and horror in a bid to appeal to a wide audience. Its international leanings have caused some Australian film scholars to regard it with ambivalence as a dilution of Australian cinema's national identity and concerns.[24] However, *Dead Calm* can also be seen as a production that aimed to celebrate Australian cinema and talent on the global stage.[25] Kidman and her Australian star persona were key to this objective; although *Dead Calm* is a three-hander, Rae Ingram is the narrative focus and, in proving herself equal if not superior to both male characters, she emerges as the lead figure. As a result, Nicole Kidman is presented as a future international star and significant Australian export.[26]

Kidman worked with Kennedy Miller again on *Flirting* (1991), John Duigan's sequel to *The Year My Voice Broke*, appearing in a relatively unsympathetic role as the beautiful but cold and sexually repressed head-prefect Nicola. Her relationship with the Kennedy Miller team resulted in acclaimed productions in which she appeared as a serious adult actress whose physical beauty and intelligence gave her star quality. She had built a reputation as a resourceful and ambitious young woman that underpinned her star persona as an example of modern Australian femininity. She had been courted by Hollywood but so far had declined offers.[27] The international success of *Dead Calm*, which hinged on her presence, piqued the interest of those involved in the big-budget Tom Cruise vehicle *Days of Thunder* (1990), directed by Tony Scott and scripted by Robert Towne, produced by Don Simpson and Jerry Bruckheimer for Paramount. Cruise and Kidman met and were immediately attracted to one another. The couple's high-profile relationship and marriage defined Kidman's career and star persona for several years to come.

An Australian in Hollywood

Legend has it that Tom Cruise 'discovered' the twenty-two-year-old Nicole Kidman and kick-started her international career. In reality Kidman was already a popular star in Australia, had a substantial list of credits and had demonstrated that she was capable of determining her future direction herself. The meeting with Cruise has been presented as a *coup de foudre* in which both were immediately smitten. Apart from their whirlwind romance, there were several factors that may have influenced Kidman's decision to accept Hollywood's offer this time. At twenty-seven, Tom Cruise was a multi-award winning actor and high-earning star, a successful product of the package system.[28] *Days of Thunder* was a big-budget production exploiting the box-office success of *Top Gun* (1986);[29] the part of Cruise's love interest Dr Claire Lewicki was not a starring role but it was significant enough to represent a stepping stone to better things; her fee, though nowhere near that earned by Cruise as Cole Trickle, was considerably higher than she was used to.[30] In terms of her star persona, the Lewicki character was an independent professional woman critical of the macho heroics of the racing circuit. The fact that she succumbed to Trickle's charms allowed Kidman's beauty and sexual charisma to be showcased, but her costume was androgynous and her mane of red hair untidy. This was not the carefully groomed style of conventional Hollywood glamour. The actress's tomboy appearance signified her newness and her difference. Her Australian accent supported this sense of cultural otherness.

The box-office and critical response to *Days of Thunder* was disappointing, though it was a modest commercial success overall.[31] Promotion focused heavily on Cruise, as did reviews, which tended to treat it as a formula movie and star vehicle.[32] If Kidman's performance was mentioned, it was noted that she had little to do in a movie that was primarily focused on the male characters. Cruise's star presence may have been overwhelming but Kidman's Claire Lewicki made her mark, not least with her forthright opinions and striking looks. In the seduction scene, she was sexually aggressive and an equal partner. As with her previous work, Kidman's rendition was naturalistic, in tune with the character; at the same time, her Australian star identity, carried over from *Dead Calm*, was evident in her depiction of Lewicki. In her next project, she took on another free-spirited role as worldly New York socialite Drew Preston opposite Dustin Hoffman as Dutch Schultz in the period gangster film, *Billy Bathgate* (1991), adapted from E. L. Doctorow's novel by Robert Benton and directed by him for Touchstone. Kidman had revealing nude scenes; her accent was now American, her red hair was tamed and her skin no longer had a hint of freckles. This transformation could be explained by the 1930s setting but it also suggested a transition from her Australian identity to a less-specific version of modern womanhood. With her adoption of an American accent, her acting appeared less naturalistic.

At the end of 1990, following Cruise's divorce from Mimi Rogers, Nicole Kidman and Tom Cruise were married in a small-scale, secret ceremony. In the face of intense media interest in their relationship, the couple retained as much privacy as they could even while they undertook extensive promotional work. Both were skilled in media interaction and adept at fielding intrusive questions from interviewers. Kidman was evidently concerned about appearing to trade on Cruise's stardom and in interviews contested the story that she was an Australian Cinderella rescued by an American Prince Charming. She stressed her Australian background and experience and foregrounded many of the elements of her Australian persona. She appeared friendly and accessible but nevertheless maintained a discreet distance when it came to discussing details of her marriage.[33] The celebrity couple presented themselves as happy and in love.[34] Kidman and Cruise avoided doing professional photo shoots together, resisting the star-couple brand and making it clear that they had independent careers. Their reticence about their relationship led to widespread speculation about the impact of Cruise's Scientology on their lives, negative comments by his ex-wife Mimi Rogers and his sexuality – rumours that were robustly denied.[35] There was a perception that Kidman was cold and aloof, perhaps deriving from her ambitious, driven persona, her cultural difference and controlled performance style.[36]

Dyer and others have pointed to the importance of secrecy, revelation and confession in making stars.[37] It is notable that while Kidman and Cruise contested the accuracy of media reports, they were aware that rumour is an important factor in such coverage. Their efforts to 'set the record straight' reinforce the idea that there are 'real' people behind the stories. At the same time, the dynamic between media gossip and star testimony throws doubt on their assertions and suggests that the rumours may have substance. The consumer is left in a position of uncertainty; curiosity, fantasy and desire drive the continual search for veracity and keep the star personas alive in the public imagination. Kidman's marriage to Tom Cruise presented her with opportunities but also with constraints. Celebrity coupledom was not always an advantage; their appearances together in *Days of Thunder* and *Far and Away* (1992) received mixed reviews, while Kidman's roles in *Malice* (1993) and *My Life* (1993) were hardly distinguished in comparison with Cruise's success in *A Few Good Men* (1992) and *The Firm* (1993). Because of their marriage, she had a high level of public visibility but this did not necessarily translate into favourable career options. In 1994, she expressed a desire to actively develop her own profile separately from her husband and to join the ranks of top female actresses such as Demi Moore, Meg Ryan and Michelle Pfeiffer.[38] In the same interview she acknowledged her resemblance to Ann-Margret and said that she had always wanted to be a 'sex-kitten'.

The idea of her resemblance to other female stars in her own search to become an icon was evident in a photo shoot she did for

Nicole Kidman imitates classic
Hollywood style (*Vogue*,
January 1994, photograph:
Rocky Schenck)

Australian *Vogue* in 1994, guest edited by Baz Luhrmann,
Catherine Martin and Bill Marron.[39] She mimicked stars of silent
and classic Hollywood cinema in a chameleon display that
foregrounded her impersonation skills.[40] This was a defining
moment apart from being her first meeting with Baz Luhrmann.
It was the beginning of a sustained drive to establish herself as
a commodity star capable of spanning different genres and
media forms. Paul McDonald points to the importance in the
contemporary industry of genre and star vehicles in setting up
audience expectation and providing coherence of star identity across
roles.[41] In the case of the modern commodity star, however, the
persona is fragmented to allow for maximum mobility and
exploitation. Kidman's persona increasingly became identified with
the adoption of multiple poses in different guises; the sheer diversity

of images and roles rendered her simultaneously ubiquitous and unknowable.[42]

In its reliance on pastiche, Kidman's commodity stardom can be seen as a postmodern phenomenon. The commodity star is market-driven and is the incarnation of the commercial imperatives of the global media industries. In Kidman's case, however, this has another dimension. The fragmentation of her image and her appropriation of different performance styles and personas can be interpreted as bringing into focus the labour involved in acting and stardom. It also draws attention to the fact that as an actress she represents the words and ideas of others rather than speaking for herself – a 'theatrical' mode that evokes Brechtian epic theatre.[43] As I discuss in the next chapter, this has postcolonial implications in so far as it represents a resistance to integration into naturalistic forms of cinematic representation.[44] Kidman's international star persona traverses a tension between commercialism and art, defined as artifice. She treads a fine line between travesty, more marked in her work with certain directors, and artistic flourish, which enables her to project herself as a star who transcends individual roles while still straddling multiple personifications.

The road to international stardom

The mid-to-late 1990s were pivotal in Kidman's progress to international stardom. In 1995 she appeared as Dr Chase Meridian in Joel Schumacher's *Batman Forever* and as fame-hungry Suzanne Stone in Gus Van Sant's satire on celebrity *To Die For*. Both characters displayed an overtly predatory sexuality and were realised by Kidman using a non-naturalistic performance style and a broad American accent with occasional undertones of an Australian twang. Her appearance changed: Dr Chase Meridian had long strawberry blonde hair reminiscent of Veronica Lake and Suzanne Stone also had smooth blonde hair. While these transformations can be put down to the demands of genre and role, they also coincided with the shifts in persona already noted. In photo shoots for *Vanity Fair* and *Vogue* at the time, images depicted Kidman in a variety of poses as a highly sexualised figure.[45] In many of the photographs, Kidman's gaze is directed at the camera, suggesting a pin-up-style invitation to the viewer. By contrast, the text of the articles emphasise her down-to-earth qualities, Australian background, professionalism and ambition while also flagging up her interest in fashion. There is a tension between the remoteness created by the posed glamour shots and the sense of accessibility and familiarity projected by the articles. Kidman's glamorisation in glossy magazine coverage was an important part of her reconstruction into an A-list star. In addition to displaying her beauty, style and sexuality, the photographs and the different personas she adopted paraded her performance skills. Increasingly, she was positioned as a leader of fashion, something to which her physique was eminently suited. This contributed to an increase in her public visibility, with her image being widely disseminated, enabling her to become a focus for fans' aspirations to emulate her looks.

The role of Suzanne Stone in *To Die For* was a turning point in her bid for stardom in her own right. Her performance as the sexually manipulative, murderous television presenter was praised by critics, some of whom commented that she had reinvented herself.[46] Others considered that she had succeeded in escaping her image as Tom Cruise's wife.[47] She was nominated for several awards and won a Golden Globe.[48] There was a general awareness in the media, no doubt nurtured by publicity machines, that Kidman was moving into a different phase as an actress. Her celebrity marriage and the rumours surrounding it continued to feature in media coverage, which returned constantly to the question of whether it was a 'marriage of convenience', fuelled by the couple's adoption of two children.[49] Elements of Kidman's persona fed into such stories and into the reception of her role in *To Die For*. There was a synergy between her highly staged, sexualised image in magazine photo shoots, her profile as a ruthlessly ambitious actress and her stylised rendition of Suzanne Stone that contributed to public perceptions of her as cynical and self-seeking even though she refuted such notions.

The critical success of *To Die For* and the acclaim for Kidman's performance paved the way for more artistically adventurous work. Although Gus Van Sant's film had been made for major studio Columbia, it was relatively modest in scale and in formal terms, it had the attributes of art cinema. Kidman's next major project was a reinterpretation of Henry James's novel *The Portrait of a Lady* directed by Jane Campion for independent companies PolyGram and Propaganda Films. She had the lead role as the idealistic, independent American heiress Isabel Archer, who finds herself trapped in a loveless marriage to the devious and mercenary Gilbert Osmond, played by John Malkovich. The production had the cultural credibility associated with a period literary adaptation and a critically esteemed director with a prestigious art-house triumph behind her.[50] Campion's treatment of the novel courted controversy by interpolating a dream sequence in which Isabel's sexual fantasies were played out. The critical response was ambivalent: many did not appreciate the changes to the novel and what was perceived as Campion and screenwriter Laura Jones's feminist 'take'. Kidman's performance was deemed good but not outstanding, with Barbara Hershey as Madame Merle gaining most attention.[51] In a *Vanity Fair* photo shoot by Annie Leibovitz, Kidman was portrayed in period costume and setting in a series of artistically framed portraits that emphasised her isolation, echoing the style of the film. The melancholy of the photographs was not evident in the accompanying article, where the actress was matter-of-fact about the critical response and professed to be proud of her work in *The Portrait of a Lady*.[52]

Artistic aspirations: Nicole Kidman in *The Portrait of a Lady*

The artistic aspirations and European flavour of *The Portrait of a Lady* strengthened Kidman's reputation as an actress and laid the foundations for more serious roles. Her next project was a very different undertaking: the action movie *The Peacemaker* (1997), the first film from Steven Spielberg's new studio DreamWorks, in which she played humourless nuclear scientist Dr Julia Kelly against George Clooney's maverick Special Forces officer. This genre outing might seem to have been a step backwards; but it was admired by some as a stylish political thriller and it opened the way for Kidman to play action heroines. Her choice of diametrically opposed ventures was no doubt strategic, intended to showcase her suitability for any vehicle. Her commitment to diversity was evident in her part as the seductive Gillian Owens in Griffin Dunne's quirky comedy *Practical Magic* (1998) and in her 1998 theatre appearance in David Hare's update of Arthur Schnitzler's erotic play *Der Reigen*, *The Blue Room*, directed by Sam Mendes. Kidman's brief nudity on stage contributed to the controversy surrounding the production, which moved to New York after a successful run in London. Apparently both Baz Luhrmann and Stephen Daldry were in the New York audience sizing up the actress for *Moulin Rouge!* (2001) and *The Hours* (2002).[53]

Kidman received critical praise and prestigious theatre award nominations for *The Blue Room*.[54] She played several roles, which demanded skilful character changes and shifts of accent. Her ability to move convincingly between pathos and comedy impressed critics as did her willingness to abandon her movie-star glamour – although it was acknowledged that her star persona was a major attraction.[55] The play consolidated her acting credentials and her flexibility, both key features in her progress to international stardom. It also dovetailed neatly into her next film project, Stanley Kubrick's *Eyes Wide Shut* (1999), based on a Schnitzler novella, in which she was playing opposite Tom Cruise. Through canny career choices, some of them controversial, she had established for herself a star identity separate from that of her husband and built a profile as an accomplished and bankable actress. Her beauty, charisma and style were widely celebrated as were her qualities of independence and risk-taking approach to life and work. She was in a position to choose projects and had optioned Susanna Moore's provocative novel, *In the Cut*, on which she planned to work again with Jane Campion.[56] She was in demand, poised to take her stardom to the next level and become an industry A-lister.

Negotiating celebrity stardom

The media exposure surrounding celebrities is generally treated with suspicion as carefully managed marketing hype controlled by the entertainment industries.[57] Intimate personal details, tragic events and private emotions are all available to be exploited for commercial gain. Fictions are created for consumers to buy into and buy. In this fluid situation, photographs can work to anchor the celebrity identity, at least temporarily.[58] As noted, the 'truth' of stars' lives and experiences is impossible to ascertain; yet a dialectic between sympathetic identification and scepticism operates between consumer and star in relation to celebrity narratives. Celebrities and publicity apparatuses are aware of and work on this dialectic to appeal to consumers, who are part of the system as they negotiate networks of 'infotainment'. The star-making process is best seen in terms of mutual transactions between different agencies, including audiences. The aims of each may be different but the labour of publicity and promotion is matched by the work of those who receive and interact with its output.

The idea of consumer interaction with the products of the star-making industries is given more credence in this era of new technologies when forms of direct access via the internet to images, news and gossip proliferate.[59] In this context, it is too pessimistic to see the publicity machinery surrounding stars as a closed regime. Whatever the efforts made to control the star-making system, there is constant leakage that threatens to destabilise it further. Stars and their publicity agents try to manage such seepage but are not always successful. An example was Tom Cruise's 2005 appearance on *The Oprah Winfrey Show* (1986–) when he jumped up and down on a couch hysterically declaring his love for Katie Holmes, setting off a deluge of media critique and public ridicule and leading to speculation about his state of mind.[60] This display may have been calculated to demonstrate that the star is human like the rest of us, but it misfired and resulted in damage to his reputation and popularity.

With respect to the rumours about their relationship, Cruise and Kidman generally appeared sanguine, even while they took time in interviews to issue denials. They seemed to accept that such gossip, though tiresome, went with the territory. However, from 1996, they hit back with a series of lawsuits against the tabloid press, including a 1998 libel action against London's Express Newspapers, which they won.[61] The reason given for the turn to litigation was the desire to protect their children.[62] The actions did not stop the rumours but they were an assertion of Cruise's star power at a time when he was consolidating his position in the industry.[63] They also coincided with the long gestation period and shooting of *Eyes Wide Shut*, a film in which the sexuality of Cruise's character Dr Bill Harford came into question. It may be too cynical to suggest that the legal actions were partly motivated by a desire to draw attention to the gossip in order to stimulate interest in the film, but that was one of the byproducts. The secrecy surrounding the production no doubt contributed to further speculation.[64] *Eyes Wide Shut* was a major undertaking for Cruise and Kidman; they accepted the terms of working with legendary perfectionist Kubrick, moving to Britain with their children for the duration. Although both had worked with high-profile directors, Kubrick was in a different league, almost a cult figure, and the project represented a departure from anything they had done previously.

Paul McDonald has described how, in the post-studio era, the package system has given renewed power to stars in attracting funding for and selling films.[65] Stars have become the key selling point for a project although their presence cannot guarantee box-office or critical success. In the case of *Eyes Wide Shut*, the participation of the Cruise/Kidman star couple brought a high-profile brand that no doubt encouraged Warner Bros to commit.[66] While each star individually would have been a significant draw, the match between the nature of the undertaking and their celebrity meant that together they were an even greater attraction. In terms of their own careers, while they sacrificed financial reward to be involved, they could expect to gain artistic kudos.[67] However, the film's release was complicated by Kubrick's death shortly after its completion and by a generally unsympathetic critical response. Cruise and Kidman's performances were not universally liked and the dissection of the central characters' marriage carried over into perceptions of the stars' precarious relationship. Although no personal difficulties were on public display, within a year they had separated.[68] Jeannette Delamoir has detailed the culture shock that resulted from the split and the maelstrom of attention devoted to the story in the media.[69]

Throughout the divorce and its aftermath, Kidman's relationship with Tom Cruise continued to feature prominently in the construction of her stardom. The reasons for the marriage breakdown remained private, which led to speculation about religion, fertility, work, sexuality and adultery as the basis for the couple's 'irreconcilable differences'. The stories were motivated by a desire to excavate the secrets behind the public façade as the divorce reignited the rumours about Cruise's homosexuality, threatening the heterosexual image central to his star persona. The couple had traded on their compatibility throughout their marriage; this construction now had to be reassessed.[70] Kidman's relationship problems became part of the story of her next production, Baz Luhrmann's *Moulin Rouge!*, as one of the factors responsible for its delay.[71] She was portrayed as emotionally devastated; her private pain was used to offer access to the 'real' person behind the fabricated image, a common device in star narratives. In this tragic scenario she appeared as a victim, a perception that complemented her role as the dying courtesan Satine in *Moulin Rouge!*.

In interviews, she gave the impression that she was more interested in marriage and family than in a successful career, counteracting notions that she was ruthlessly ambitious. She confessed to fears that the divorce would mean that she would no longer be offered work but, in fact, she now entered the most productive phase of her career. While media coverage focused on her emotional struggles, she was also projected as a courageous single woman on a journey to reinvent herself personally and professionally.[72] The shifts in Kidman's persona at this time positioned her as a vulnerable human being, encouraging empathy with her and strengthening her authenticity. A 2002 *Vanity Fair* photo shoot displayed her in freewheeling, intimate poses far removed from the carefully staged, distant shots through which she was previously portrayed. Once again, contradictions emerged between text and image, as the mature sensibility evident in the interview conflicted with the girlish exuberance of the photographs.[73]

In working with Kubrick, she and Cruise had made a strategic decision to immerse themselves in a particular creative process in order to associate themselves with an auteur whose films were far from mainstream. In today's industry, alliance with critically revered directors enhances stars' prestige. It also enables them to increase their range by crossing over between commercially driven movies and the art-cinema market, which has burgeoned with the expansion of independent production and distribution companies and the

After Tom: a new Nicole
Kidman emerges (*Vanity Fair*,
December 2002, photograph:
Mario Testino)

emergence of the 'major independents', or 'mini majors', in the
1990s.[74] While art-house projects usually promise modest financial
rewards, they enable those involved to acquire 'creative capital' that
gives them leverage in negotiations with industry agencies.[75] Over the
next four years, Kidman concentrated on building her art-cinema
profile by taking on artistically adventurous projects, starting with
the risky venture *Moulin Rouge!*, a reinvention of the classic musical.
Her performance was often histrionic, in keeping with Baz
Luhrmann's operatic rendition of the story; this and her singing were
well received, despite a mixed critical response to the film. In *The
Others* (*Los otros*, 2001), Alejandro Amenábar's disturbing depiction
of a mother's unravelling psyche, produced by Cruise/Wagner
Productions, she also triumphed; the soundtrack for this and for the
low-budget British comedy *Birthday Girl* (2001), in which she played
a Russian con-artist, included music numbers sung by Kidman.[76]

Her roles in these titles effectively showcased her acting abilities; but it was with her appearance as Virginia Woolf in Stephen Daldry's *The Hours* that she staked her claim to full-blown artistic credibility. Another prestigious literary adaptation, scripted by David Hare from Michael Cunningham's novel, the film dealt with the impact of Woolf's novel *Mrs Dalloway* on three generations of women. Kidman underwent a radical transformation for the part, wearing a prosthetic nose and altering the timbre of her voice.[77] Daldry's subtle direction and Kidman's performance were widely admired and she won three major Best Actress awards, including her first and only Oscar to date. The next year she was rewarded with a star in the Hollywood Walk of Fame. The critical and box-office success of *The Hours* was followed by a trio of very different projects, from Lars von Trier's experimental *Dogville* to Robert Benton's adaptation of Philip Roth's dark novel *The Human Stain* and Anthony Minghella's epic Civil War Western, *Cold Mountain*, also a literary adaptation (all 2003). *The Hours*, *Dogville* and *Cold Mountain* could be described as ensemble pieces: each featured a company of respected actors rather than spotlighting individual star performers. Kidman was not successful in all cases in immersing her star identity in the characters she portrayed but such projects were nevertheless important in enhancing her profile as a talented actress willing to embrace challenging work. During this prolific period, interview material often focused on Kidman's approach to performance, noting her acting achievements.[78]

Her style and fashion sense became an increasingly prominent feature of her persona and she was depicted as being as elegant in casual sportswear as in *haute couture*.[79] Her association with leading fashion brands such as Dior, Chanel and Yves Saint Laurent was important in projecting the star as a glamour icon as her ever-changing 'look' adorned the covers of fashion and lifestyle magazines with greater frequency. The links between fashion and cinema are not new. Since the 1910s, stars have paraded designer clothes on and off screen, displaying glamour and conspicuous consumption to draw audiences.[80] The spectacular dimension of fashion carries over to the stars' appearances on the red carpet at awards ceremonies, which can be seen as a kind of catwalk. It is here that stars showcase their carefully groomed façades and the exotic products of designer brands.[81] Fashion's preoccupation with beauty, spectacle and the performance of identity is tied in with the commodity star's presence in different guises across multiple commercial events. These images are obsessively examined, particularly in the celebrity press, which delights in pointing out fashion *faux pas* and printing candid shots that capture the star at their worst. This response often appears purely malicious but it also works to deconstruct the manufacture of beauty at the heart of commodity stardom.[82] Since the mid-2000s, Kidman's appearance has repeatedly been the target of negative commentary. As she reached her late thirties, attention focused more and more on the steps she took to remain looking young, with widespread tabloid speculation about her use of Botox and plastic surgery. Her denials simply intensified the rumours.

Kidman's charisma and status as a fashion trendsetter had other repercussions, as in some films, her appearance singled her out from other cast members. Her beauty as Ada in *Cold Mountain* or janitor Faunia Farley in *The Human Stain* was perceived by some as a drawback, in that it gave the character too much star lustre in contrast to her plainness as Virginia Woolf.[83] In 2004 she became the face of the iconic perfume Chanel No. 5, which has historically been linked with female stars, and appeared in a commercial for the fragrance directed by Baz Luhrmann in which she played a glamorous celebrity desperate to find refuge from the demands of her fame.[84] The same year she starred in *Birth*, Jonathan Glazer's unsettling meditation on the effects of grief, in which her character Anna believes that her dead husband is reincarnated in the form of a young boy. The project was high risk; apart from its downbeat subject matter and opaque narrative structure, it included a

Seeking commercial success: Nicole Kidman in
The Stepford Wives

controversial scene in which she took a bath with the boy. Her
cropped hair and gamine looks were striking, bringing Hollywood-
style glitz to an art-house project. *Birth* and Kidman's performance
were appreciated by some,[85] but the film was not a critical or
commercial success. This, following the mediocre showing of *Cold
Mountain* and *The Human Stain*, may have motivated her change of
direction. She embarked on a series of more mainstream star vehicles
beginning with *The Stepford Wives* (2004), Frank Oz's remake of the
classic 1975 film, followed by Sydney Pollack's political thriller *The
Interpreter* (2005) and Nora Ephron's update of the popular 1960s
television comedy series *Bewitched*, also 2005.

In 2006, Kidman was listed as Hollywood's highest-paid
actress, overtaking Julia Roberts who had held the top spot for five
years.[86] Approaching forty, she was at the peak of her career and had
achieved the powerful A-list status to which she aspired. She had
made strategic, occasionally perilous, professional decisions that

resulted in her becoming the ultimate commodity star/celebrity, a box-office draw and a respected actress. One such risk-laden decision was to take the part of Diane Arbus in Steven Shainberg's fictional tribute to the troubled photographer *Fur: An Imaginary Portrait of Diane Arbus* (2006); the film and her performance were poorly received by many critics.[87] She had met and married her second husband, country singer Keith Urban. She was awarded the high honour of Companion of the Order of Australia and became UNIFEM Goodwill Ambassador. She had set up her own production company Blossom Films and secured a three-year, first-look deal with 20th Century Fox.[88] These were remarkable personal and professional achievements; yet within two years, following a string of commercial failures, she was described as 'box-office poison', while her performances in films such as Baz Luhrmann's historical epic *Australia* (2008) were derided.[89]

Rise, fall and rise again

A star's career can founder as a result of poor professional choices. Although the modern package system has brought stars more freedom and power, it also means that their success is directly tied to the theatrical and ancillary revenues attained by their films. Since the star's value lies in their potential as a box-office draw, one or two commercial failures can cause their popularity to falter and their bankability to decline.[90] In a competitive freelance market, the more films a star makes, the more likely it is that one or two will be successful and help to counteract the effect of any that fail at the box office. In Kidman's case, between 2004 and 2007 she appeared in eight titles that under-performed at the box office on their initial release: *The Stepford Wives, Birth, The Interpreter, Bewitched, Fur, The Invasion* (2007), *Margot at the Wedding* (2007) and *The Golden Compass* (2007). This list consisted of a mix of quasi-mainstream and adventurous art-house projects from which financial rewards and/or critical approval could have been expected. It is an indication of the instability of the contemporary star system that the predicted outcomes did not materialise, with the result that Kidman dropped out of the 2008 list of Hollywood's highest-earning actresses where the top spot was taken by Angelina Jolie.[91]

Although critical response does not necessarily determine a film's reception by audiences, it can be a significant factor in influencing the reputation of a project. The antagonistic critical reaction in the US media to Baz Luhrmann's *Australia*, much of which focused on Kidman's performance as Lady Sarah Ashley, picked up momentum across the world and led to the movie being widely proclaimed a disaster even though this was far from the case.[92] The antipathy was by no means universal but through a process of repetition facilitated by electronic communication technologies it became accepted wisdom. Kidman's status as an actress suffered as a result; although she was an Oscar-winner, she was deemed no longer able to command $10 million per movie. With the increasing focus on her age, she took on work such as the voice of 'Norma Jean' in Kennedy Miller's animated penguin musical, *Happy Feet* (2006), for which she imitated Marilyn Monroe, and acted as narrator for the documentaries *I Have Never Forgotten You: The Life and Legacy of Simon Wiesenthal* (2007) and *God Grew Tired of Us: The Story of Lost Boys of Sudan* (2006). Between 2005 and 2009, she appeared in commercials and media campaigns for Omega watches, Nintendo and Schweppes. In 2008, she and Keith Urban had their first child, which contributed to maintaining her visibility in the press. While her earning power from movies may have been temporarily reduced, her commodity stardom and celebrity profile were not diminished.

Kidman was not alone in facing a drop in earnings. According to some reports, the global recession and a sharp decline in DVD revenues had a detrimental effect on star salaries, forcing them to take pay cuts.[93] It was also claimed that A-list stars could no longer guarantee box-office success, with the result that studios were not prepared to pay the high fees they demanded. These developments led to suggestions that the star system was in crisis.[94] Kidman's financial fortunes did dip a little: in 2009, *Forbes* magazine ranked her eighth in its list of top-earning actresses, citing her appearance in *Australia* as responsible.[95] In 2010, she failed to make the *Forbes* list.[96] She was still extremely wealthy and an international star with a huge fan base;[97] nevertheless, she had received a substantial amount of negative press in response to her performances in films such as *The Invasion* and *Australia*, while Rob Marshall's musical tribute to Fellini, *Nine* (2009), in which she had a cameo role as Daniel Day-Lewis's muse, was panned. The celebrity media obsession with the impact of ageing on the actress surfaced in the quality press, with frequent comments about her wrinkle-free forehead and her lack of facial expression.[98] Her presumed use of Botox was deemed to have a detrimental effect on her acting by immobilising her features.

Kidman continued to deny using Botox and in interviews shrugged off concerns about ageing.[99] However, her denials in the face of visible evidence to the contrary worked against her and provoked more criticism. She still received positive coverage, particularly in glossy magazines such as *Vogue* and *Vanity Fair*,[100] but a tide of opinion had turned against her. With respect to her personal life, her marriage and family appeared in public to be happy and settled after she and Keith Urban had been through his spell in rehab. Her professional problems may have been virtual rather than real; nevertheless, a number of factors, including her age, swings in audience perception, shifts in the industry and the economic climate, created the need for a change of direction. In 2010, amid reports that her career was in deep trouble, Kidman left premier Hollywood agency CAA and hired a manager in addition to changing her long-term publicist.[101] With the release of *Rabbit Hole* (2010), Blossom Films' first production, in which she played a mother stricken with

"KIDMAN IS UTTERLY MESMERISING...
HER FINEST EVER PERFORMANCE"

"A FILM OF STAGGERING INSIGHT
AND BEAUTY... FLAWLESS"

NICOLE   AARON   DIANNE
KIDMAN   ECKHART   WIEST

RABBIT
HOLE

The only way out is through

Return to form: Nicole Kidman's passion
project *Rabbit Hole*

grief over the death of her son, she appeared to have turned a corner
as her performance was widely applauded by critics and she received
an Academy Award nomination for Best Actress. In 2011, she
admitted to using Botox but claimed to have given it up.[102] In a 2011
fashion shoot for *Harper's Bazaar*, she appeared in a succession of
glamorous designer dresses against a lush, romantic background in
shots that portrayed her as a natural beauty. In the same issue, an
interview with Kidman by Jennifer Aniston, her co-star in the Adam
Sandler relationship comedy *Just Go with It* (2011), mentioned the
rural charm of her home in Nashville, Tennessee and she asserted
that she was no longer as interested as she had been in high
fashion.[103]

Kidman's 'return to nature' and her new 'look' were generally
appreciated, though some expressed scepticism.[104] *Rabbit Hole*, on

which she was credited as producer, was presented as a passion project, in which she was deeply involved from its conception. This and other ventures developed by Blossom that she planned to star in and produce, such as *The Danish Girl*, based on David Ebershoff's novel inspired by the artist Einar Wegener, who underwent sex reassignment surgery to become a woman, boosted her creative capital in the industry. Her profile as a feminist role model was strengthened when she spoke out in support of UNIFEM's campaign to end violence against women, while her surprise announcement of the birth of her second child with Urban via a surrogate indicated her determination to overcome fertility problems.[105] Kidman and her publicists negotiated her career downturn by reinventing her brand. Although she did not win the Best Actress Oscar, which went to Natalie Portman for her role in *Black Swan* (2010), the favourable reception for *Rabbit Hole* and her performance were viewed as heralding a change in her fortunes, though it was recognised that much still depended on her ability to secure future hits.[106] Kidman's international stardom proved remarkably resilient in the face of industry instability and the unpredictable nature of public affection. Core elements of her persona such as her independence, intelligence and resourcefulness were brought to the fore while other aspects such as her ruthless ambition were softened in favour of philanthropic activities and a life less dominated by the glare of publicity. Her multifaceted identity was sufficiently mobile to allow for the necessary realignment with a different zeitgeist. Although her professional situation remained uncertain in a precarious business, she had demonstrated a capacity for survival.

2 PERFORMANCE

Acting and stardom, art and commerce

Stars are, of course, actors on and off screen. Many are trained for the theatre and some alternate between stage and film appearances. However, actors are not always stars, even if they have leading roles. Theatre acting carries cultural kudos, which can mean that in order to gain a reputation as a serious actor a film performer must be seen to resist the 'superficial' glamour and commercialism of the star system. Some achieve both stardom and acting credibility: Marlon Brando, for example. Others, such as Marilyn Monroe, struggle to be perceived as good actors but are defined primarily in terms of their star quality. For Charlie Chaplin, it was his character the Tramp that rose to stardom, while after becoming famous John Wayne was primarily 'John Wayne' no matter which character he played.[1] Today, respected actors such as Robert De Niro or Al Pacino, who are identified with certain genres and directors and have developed recognisable performance repertoires, have acquired star status because of their skill in character parts. Their participation in commodity stardom and celebrity brouhaha is limited, which adds to their esteem. It is more difficult for A-list stars, whose value lies in their capacity to sell films and related products to as many audiences as possible, to gain acting prestige; if they succeed in doing so, it is usually because they demonstrate their willingness to immerse themselves in highbrow material. Popular entertainment is generally perceived as incompatible with serious acting.[2]

In practice, there is no hard and fast division between an actor's on-screen roles and their wider public persona; both depend on performance and the adoption of a character, although the skills deployed in acting for the cinema are more highly esteemed and have received more critical attention than those used in interactions with the media.[3] James Naremore and others have argued that professional acting is related to the role-playing that characterises everyday social behaviour and presentations of self.[4] This opens up new areas for the study of performance beyond the confines of the film text; the poses, gestures, costume, make-up, props, scripted dialogue and photographic *mise en scène* that constitute the star interview and photo shoot are ripe for analysis and reveal much about the transactions of modern stardom. Just as publicity and promotion involve acting skills as well as many other forms of labour, so the business of being a star requires work. Star quality is sometimes thought of as indefinable, a 'something extra' possessed by certain actors that singles them out from the crowd. Yet this charisma, which resides in the aura of their physical presence and in their photogenic allure, is manufactured via different kinds and degrees of technical intervention, including performance techniques.

The study of performance enables a broader conception of acting that includes all the arenas in which stars practise their craft. It is particularly useful in approaching the work of a star/celebrity/ actress such as Nicole Kidman, whose activity as a performer extends over many different media sites. Most studies of performance focus on the details of on-screen acting and in this chapter, I shall explore Kidman's evolving style as an actress through case studies of key titles in her career, leaving her performances outside film to the next chapter. While it is difficult to separate out the complex interactions between films and related media in the contemporary global entertainment industries, a close consideration of selected scenes can be useful in illuminating aspects of the star system as well as the mechanics of Kidman's acting. The framework for my discussion is the distinction often drawn between Stanislavskian naturalism, in which the actor aspires to authenticity by drawing on their inner self and emotional experience, and Brechtian didactic modernism, in which the actor emphasises the artificiality of performance in order to foster critical awareness. As scholars have noted, these two traditions are not mutually exclusive;[5] but the tension between them has proved productive in the analysis of cinema acting, where naturalistic conventions are generally prized and more histrionic styles are either deemed bad technique or confined to specialist areas.[6]

The quality of Kidman's acting is a topic that provokes widespread debate among critics, fans and online forums. It is not unusual for stars to attract assessment of their performance skills; such considerations are central to audience response and critical evaluations of acting are frequently used to market films.[7] Indeed, it can be argued that viewer interaction plays an important part in producing performance. In Kidman's case, it is striking that opinion is often deeply divided and, when it comes to negative response, sometimes expressed with intensity and malice.[8] Certain performances, such as those in which she is perceived to be at one with the character, are lauded, whereas those in which her acting is deemed non-authentic are denigrated. Her work with acclaimed directors might be well received while more controversial or routine productions might provoke antagonism. The sharp division of opinion is a sign of the capriciousness of the contemporary industry in which the critical and box-office success of a project is rarely guaranteed and failure is attributed to the star even if they are not responsible. It is also a symptom of Kidman's position as a commodity star, who lays claim to being a serious actress. This contradiction is difficult to accommodate in the context of the opposition between art and commerce in conceptions of screen acting. There is also the issue of Kidman's perceived difficulty in connecting with audiences: she is often described as lacking the 'likeability factor'.[9] Performance is directed at viewers; it is essential to engaging them in the aesthetic experience of the film. A dialogue exists between the construction of character and audience expectations, which often have moral and ethical dimensions.[10] If the dialogue fails, for whatever reason, the performer usually suffers the consequences. By looking at the development of Kidman's acting over time, I shall attempt to throw light on the assumptions underlying the judgments brought to bear on her performance and the extent to which they determine her relationship with audiences. I shall also explore the wider implications of screen performance.

Dead Calm (Phillip Noyce, 1989)

Dead Calm was an Australian production from the Kennedy Miller team, which was responsible for the acclaimed television miniseries *Vietnam* (1987) in which Nicole Kidman portrayed Megan Goddard's progression from awkward teenager to free-thinking young woman. Kidman won an Australian Film Institute (AFI) award for her performance; one powerful scene in which she protests against conscription on a radio programme and then breaks down when her brother, a recently returned veteran, rings in, influenced the makers of *Dead Calm* to cast her as Rae Ingram, wife of Sam Neill's naval captain John Ingram. Kidman was twenty when casting began and was deemed too young for the part of a woman in her thirties. However, the older, more experienced actresses approached, including Sigourney Weaver and Debra Winger, declined and, despite the age difference between herself and the forty-year-old Neill, Kidman got the role.[11] Scriptwriter Terry Hayes made adjustments to Charles Williams's source novel to accommodate Kidman's participation. He added a backstory in which the couple's reason for taking a voyage across the Pacific in their yacht *Saracen* was the death of their son in a car accident while Rae was driving. This trauma became the focus of the tensions between the two troubled characters who are unable to come to terms with the past.[12] John Ingram's control of the situation is threatened by the intrusion of psychopathic killer Hughie Warriner, played by up-and-coming American actor Billy Zane, who boards the *Saracen* after fleeing the grisly mass murders he has carried out on his boat *Orpheus*. John, doubting Hughie's food-poisoning story, investigates the *Orpheus* and becomes trapped. During his absence, Hughie takes over the *Saracen* and threatens Rae's life; she finally overcomes him and, after setting his body adrift in the ocean, rescues her husband. However, Hughie is not dead and boards the *Saracen* once more, to be killed by John.

Kidman carried out extensive research for her role as Rae, who goes from childlike dependency on her husband to resourceful survivor and equal partner in the course of the story. According to Noyce, she studied posture in order to carry herself like a thirty-year-old woman who had had a child and undertook training to make herself sound older by dropping the pitch of her voice.[13] She put on weight and devoted considerable time to conjuring up emotions of maternal grief.[14] Noyce's working method was to encourage thorough preparation before shooting began to ensure that characterisation was in place in advance and he only had to 'nudge' the actors on set.[15] The film is character led, using close-ups of the actors' expressions to impart a sense of unease. There is not a great deal of dialogue, so that thoughts, feelings and motivations remain open to interpretation. One example is a close shot early on in which John watches Rae from the yacht as she swims languorously in the sea. The camera lingers on his gaze, which appears to be loving and also seems to express sexual longing. As his eyes narrow, John's look at his wife moves from tenderness to unspoken anger and hardens into a desire for control. This slight change of expression intimates the problems in their relationship that the narrative works to resolve.

Both Kidman and Neill give understated performances but Neill's portrayal of John is exceptionally contained, depicting his unwillingness to allow emotions to surface.

The unacknowledged tensions in the Ingrams' marriage are grotesquely mirrored in Rae's struggle with the monstrous Hughie. Zane's hyperbolic rendition contrasts with Neill's restraint; he overtly displays the emotional chaos that John suppresses. As John discovers the horrors on board the *Orpheus* and tries to warn his wife about the danger she faces, Rae becomes locked in a violent conflict with the killer played out in the confined spaces of the yacht. After failing to overcome her attacker, Rae decides to change tack. She deceives Hughie into believing that she wants to be friends and allows him to seduce her in order to disarm him. In the seduction sequence, Kidman performs for Hughie as well as for the cinema audience as she pretends to enjoy their encounter while her expression indicates that she is in distress. The scene is replete with irony; although the sex is consensual it takes place under duress, suggesting rape. Because of Rae's deception, Hughie believes that she enjoys it although the viewer knows that she does not. Rae's disgust is evident; nevertheless, the sex with Hughie energises her into taking actions that finally defeat him. Throughout the scene, she is depicted as an active participant rather than a victim as she takes control of the situation.

The seduction begins as Rae is weeping in the cabin, having failed to make contact with John on the *Orpheus* via the radio. Hughie approaches her, kisses and touches her with tenderness as though to comfort her. There is no dialogue, only the faint sound of the characters' breathing. Rae appears childlike at first; initially she reacts to Hughie with a tremulous smile as if welcoming his actions but as he proceeds she responds to his actions with curiosity. These moments are ambiguous; she does not attempt to stop him and she seems to acquiesce to his advances. But when he embraces her, a big close-up of Kidman's face as she looks into camera over his shoulder shows a cold, calculating expression that indicates her intentions.

Challenge to Hollywood: Nicole Kidman and
Billy Zane in *Dead Calm*

The youth of the actors is important at this point. Both seem
vulnerable; Hughie is transformed from violent aggressor to gentle
lover while Rae changes from frightened child to resolute woman.
This results in a shift of sympathy towards Hughie. Despite the
danger posed to Rae by Hughie, his willingness to believe that she
is attracted to him puts him at a disadvantage. As Rae takes control
and Hughie takes the position of victim he becomes more human.
Kidman's performance is vital to regaining audience sympathy for
Rae. At the beginning of the sex scene, Rae is on top of Hughie but
she breaks away, claiming that she needs to go to the bathroom. She
puts on a short bathrobe and secretly goes to find a weapon stored on
deck. The weapon does not work and she is frightened and panicky,
which increases suspense and encourages identification with her.
When Hughie comes to find Rae, she adopts a confident pose and
pretends to have been looking for a pack of cigarettes. When the sex

resumes, Hughie is on top and the camera focuses on Kidman's expressions, which indicate her anguish to the viewer, though Hughie remains oblivious. Afterwards, Rae is shown in medium shot sitting on the end of the bed, staring into space as her face sets into a desire for revenge.

Through Rae's subterfuge, a divide occurs between the character's acting for another character in the fiction and Kidman's acting directed at the audience, which has superior knowledge of what is going on. The character is positioned as an actress, so that Kidman's performance skills are to the fore. It is Rae's deception that ultimately enables her to overcome Hughie and the film can be seen to be about performance on the levels of narrative and acting. Because of the paucity of dialogue in the seduction sequence, suspense, identification and comprehension depend on the expressive techniques used by the actors through gesture, gaze, facial expression, body movement and voice. They remain in character and do not display rhetorical or theatrical flourishes in these scenes; nevertheless, there is an ostensive dimension to their acting because the situation depends on performance. Their naturalistic method here co-exists with a drive to presentation, inflecting the usual distinction drawn between ostensiveness and understatement in acting styles.[16] The film's focus on performance has implications for national cinema and identity. As noted, there is a marked difference between the restrained acting of the Australian couple and the showy histrionics of the American character, who is ultimately eliminated. This implies a challenge to the global power of Hollywood. In her role as Rae, Kidman is deglamorised, in contrast to Zane's pretty-boy appearance. Her tomboy sexuality, familiar from her earlier parts, chimes with that of Hollywood action heroines, such as Ripley (Sigourney Weaver) in *Alien* (1979) or Sarah Connor (Linda Hamilton) in *The Terminator* (1984), lining her up as a future Australian export.

In this context, the fact that Kidman is seen to be assuming roles in *Dead Calm* (the façade she presents to her husband; the ruse she adopts for Hughie) has further ramifications. The struggle of Australia's postcolonial society to forge new histories, languages and forms of expression can be seen in the drive of its national cinema to fracture, appropriate and deconstruct the representational modes of the ruling cultures.[17] In Australian cinema's complex response to the global domination of Hollywood, the drive to differentiate itself produces aesthetic strategies that recast and dramatise that relationship.[18] One of the markers of Kidman's identity as a non-Hollywood actress in this film is the presentation of her as performing a part not only for the film's characters but also for Australian and American audiences. While this tactic does not approach the epic address of Brechtian theatre, which creates a schism between actor and character,[19] it produces a sense that she is in disguise and that her 'true', authentic self is constantly in the process of revision. Following her move to Hollywood, this trait increasingly became a feature of Kidman's persona and her performances. Her adoption of a series of masks not only signifies her own alienation; it can also alienate audience sympathy and identification, as I demonstrated in my analysis of the seduction sequence. Sympathy is only re-engaged when the mask is dropped. *Dead Calm* received several AFI technical awards but none of the actors was nominated. The film was not universally liked by US critics, some of whom perceived it as exploitation fare, but it was successful enough to propel both Kidman and Noyce to Hollywood.[20] In Kidman's case, it paved the way for her US debut as Dr Claire Lewicki opposite Tom Cruise in *Days of Thunder* (1990).

To Die For (Gus Van Sant, 1995)

The acerbic black comedy *To Die For*, scripted by Buck Henry from Joyce Maynard's novel about a young woman's fatal addiction to celebrity, represented the launch of Kidman's bid for international stardom following a series of supporting roles that did little to enhance her reputation as a serious actress.[21] The film was made for Columbia Pictures, which considered it too bleak to be a major success and was surprised when it became a hit. Its production and release coincided with the media circus surrounding O. J. Simpson's televised trial for murder; the film's timeliness, together with its positive reception at the 1995 Cannes Film Festival, contributed to its favourable showing at the box office and critical acclaim.[22] Kidman's artful turn as Suzanne Stone Maretto, who is obsessed with becoming a television personality and arranges the murder of her husband when he gets in the way of her ambitions, was singled out by some as potentially Oscar-winning.[23] Kidman is certainly positioned as a star by the film; but it is misleading to attribute this entirely to her acting skills, important though they are. *To Die For* puts on display the plethora of elements that combine to produce screen performance.

Philip Drake makes the point that, despite the emphasis on intentionality in studies of acting, the creation of character and narrative coherence in movies is better seen as an effect of a number of factors, among which the performer's use of expressive techniques is only one. The actor's deployment of performance skills via their body is mediated by editing and framing, or by their relationship with other actors. What is perceived as the presence of the actor on screen is actually the result of technical intervention. Following Naremore, Drake acknowledges the preference for representational acting, which is less ostensive and effaces the production of performance, in narrative cinema.[24] Representational acting encourages the sense that the performance is the product of the actor's intentions, a perception that is reinforced by accounts of their preparations for the role. The focus on Kidman's Suzanne Stone in critical response to *To Die For* was supported by reports of her hard work and thorough research from the director.[25] There were also stories that she had approached Van Sant directly to convince him that she should be given the part.[26] Kidman promoted the idea that Suzanne was her creation by claiming that she sequestered herself in a hotel room for several days watching television and spoke exclusively in an American accent until the film was finished in order to fully inhabit the character.[27] Without doubt, Kidman's acting skills were vital to her bravura rendition of Suzanne and to audience assessment of her star potential. However, the film's emphasis on style makes it clear that her performance emerges from the interaction of creative and technical factors that include not only the acting of others but also narrative structure, dialogue, music, editing, framing, costume, make-up, sets, lighting and colour. These contributing elements are overtly presented to viewers and could be described as performative or ostensive in themselves.

To Die For adopts the narrative conventions of Maynard's novel, in which events are related by characters who know Suzanne and in flashback. The film mocks documentary-interview devices, using first-person direct address to camera as well as sequences staged in a television studio. In between these framing scenes, Suzanne's story is told in third-person mode, presented in fragments. This fractured structure mimics the episodic forms of television and pastiches the media barrage of celebrity culture. Irony is present at every level; yet despite the film's knowingness, a sense of authenticity and a degree of empathy are generated through the actors' performances, which mix sly comedy with ingenuousness and emotion. This creates a multilayered texture in which audience reaction to the characters shifts between contempt, sympathy, malicious pleasure, aesthetic delight and moral superiority. The primary tactic is to play off Kidman's ostensive acting style against the more naturalistic approaches of the supporting players. However, because Suzanne is constantly aware of being watched and is always performing, Kidman's acting does not break with character. Even so, it is sufficiently stylised to enable a critical distance between viewer and character while simultaneously allowing for admiration of the performance. Equally,

Nicole Kidman clowns as Suzanne Stone in *To Die For*

the naturalism used by the actors who depict the Italian-American Maretto family is both representational, remaining within the bounds of narrative, and ostensive in that it consciously draws on ethnic stereotypes. The three teenagers lured by Suzanne into her murder plot are portrayed as lumpen slackers using an exaggerated realism that is both alienating and affecting, especially in the case of Joaquin Phoenix's compelling rendition of the hapless Jimmy, who fires the shot that kills Suzanne's husband, Larry (Matt Dillon).

Kidman's characterisation of Suzanne presents her as a ruthlessly ambitious narcissist enthralled by an image-obsessed media culture. The script hints at resemblances with Kidman's own status as a celebrity and the idea that the actress was playing a version of herself was put forward by some critics.[28] Kidman infuses the character with vanity, innocence, unscrupulous cunning and lunacy all at once. The comedic dimension of her performance often produces a sense that she is clowning. In an early confessional sequence delivered direct to camera, she is brightly lit against a white background, framed in close-up so that her facial expressions and head movements dominate the screen. Her appearance gives the impression that she has tailored her 'look' for the camera; her make-up is a little too much, her smooth hairstyle resembles a wig, her jacket is a sickly shade of pink and her gilt jewellery verges on tawdry. Kidman adopts an intimate mode of address; at the same time she is clearly playing a part, so that Suzanne and the intimacy are revealed as fake.[29] Her features are mobile as she executes a number of expressions, including nods to camera, that imply she is confiding in the viewer. She smiles frequently, revealing her small white teeth in an effort to impart approachability; this gives her a slightly predatory air. She widens her eyes, which are unnaturally bright and, like her jewellery, reflect a spotlight. The dialogue, which reveals her shallowness, is delivered in a near-faultless American accent that is just false enough to remind us that Kidman is acting. Her diction is precise and at times her voice drops to a confidential whisper; the register of her voice, her intonation and speech patterns recall the carefully crafted tones of Ann-Margret or Marilyn Monroe.[30]

The sequence is cut against flashbacks and an interview scene featuring Larry's sister (Illeana Douglas), who is pictured in a noisy ice rink. The lighting, sound and Douglas's delivery are in naturalistic mode and her hair, make-up and costume are frumpy in contrast to Suzanne's contrived glamour, endowing the character with an authenticity that Suzanne lacks and generating empathy with her. On the other hand, Kidman's portrayal of the monstrous Suzanne produces an ambivalent response in the viewer, who is caught between derision for the character and admiration for the execution of the role. This ambivalence is fostered not just by Kidman's acting skills but also by the framing devices used by the film-makers. *To Die For* is presented as a collaborative ensemble work in which every component contributes to the overall result. Nevertheless, it was Kidman's performance that attracted most critical attention. She gained a host of award nominations for Best Actress and won several, including a Golden Globe.[31] Her success was double-edged; elements of her persona played on by the film such as her driving ambition, coldness and immersion in celebrity media culture became more strongly associated with her, demonstrating the dialectic between filmic characterisation and public self in cinema stardom.

Eyes Wide Shut (Stanley Kubrick, 1999)

In its conscious presentation of acting skills, Kidman's performance in *To Die For* verged on Brechtian epic style, in which character is shown rather than embodied.[32] The high degree of artifice in Kidman's rendition of Suzanne Stone produced a sense that her interpretation was manufactured. As if to compensate for the loss of authenticity, some critics put forward the notion that Kidman was playing herself; that is, her fictional persona, perceived as embodying her real self. The fusion of Kidman's public identity with the character gave Suzanne substance as an individualised person rather than allowing the character to be perceived as pure image. The interplay between persona and character is key to anchoring the protean fictions of performance in reality and giving them origins; not only do elements of star personas feed into and provide continuity between their different roles but their on-screen characters also inform the media stories featuring their public personas. This dialectic was strongly in evidence in *Eyes Wide Shut*, in which Tom Cruise and Nicole Kidman play a married couple whose relationship is in trouble. The rumours surrounding their celebrity coupledom were reactivated in media coverage of the production, while the script by Stanley Kubrick and Frederic Raphael dramatised components of their public image.

The unusual circumstances in which *Eyes Wide Shut* was made have been extensively written about.[33] The aura of secrecy surrounding the film, its supposedly sensational content and the death of director Kubrick just as it was finished added to its cult reputation. The fact that both lead actors were major Hollywood stars raised questions about their ability to deliver convincing performances in a work that, although made for Warner Bros, was decidedly non-mainstream. Kubrick was determined to use actors who were married to one another in the roles of Dr Bill Harford and his wife Alice. During the protracted gestation period, he courted Cruise and Kidman, convincing them to sign open-ended contracts and devote themselves to a production process lasting more than two years that required them to move their family to England where the director was based.[34] He demanded total dedication and the relationship between director and actors became intense and intimate.[35] Kubrick's working method involved lengthy rehearsals and multiple takes; according to Kidman, he shot some of the sexually explicit scenes personally with only himself and the actors present.[36] Cruise and Kidman were evidently in awe of Kubrick; this helps to explain their willingness to comply with his regime and to allow him to portray their marriage in a less than flattering light.[37] Strategically, they could expect to gain artistic kudos from the project to compensate for diminished financial rewards.

The script is an adaptation of Arthur Schnitzler's 1926 novella *Traumnovelle*, set in *fin-de-siècle* Vienna, which explores the obsessive jealousy of a respectable doctor who is spurred by his wife's erotic fantasies to become involved in a series of unconsummated sexual adventures. Kubrick and Raphael updated the story to modern-day New York, much of which was reconstructed at Pinewood Studios, lending the setting a sense of unreality. The film has attracted scholarly attention as an example of Kubrick's distinctive approach to acting.[38] For Dennis Bingham, the stylised performances, depicting the characters as players in an elaborate masquerade, typify a Brechtian technique that eschews psychological depth in favour of an alienation effect that prevents the viewer from becoming absorbed in the fiction.[39] By refusing the illusionism of naturalistic narrative cinema, the film presents itself as performance and problematises the relationship between art and reality.[40] The presence of Cruise and Kidman is pivotal to this operation, as their star personas and the connections between the story and their real-life situation provide further layers of fabrication. The actors portray themselves while also portraying Bill and Alice; both are presented as roles, evacuating the real people supposed to lie behind the characters. The episodic, repetitive narrative and the non-naturalistic execution of the lines by the actors contribute to a dreamlike ambience in which both players and viewers are positioned in a state between sleeping and waking.

Kubrick and Raphael's script emphasised the power struggle and gender divide at the heart of the story. Bill's actions are a direct response to his wife's criticism of his attitude towards women and her confession of an erotic fantasy in which she has sex with a young naval officer she glimpses in a hotel lobby. The film can be seen as a

An elaborate masquerade: Nicole Kidman in
Eyes Wide Shut

dissection of male heterosexual desire viewed from Bill's perspective. His sexual exploits result in a series of unsettling encounters in which he never achieves control; Alice, on the other hand, wields considerable power in a film in which women are seen to be controlled by men. Not only does she provoke Bill's fruitless search for sexual mastery but it is through her visualisation of his humiliation that his powerlessness is revealed. At the end of the film there is no doubt that she is in a dominant position; by implication, this is the way Bill wants her to be. The scene in which Alice confronts her husband, threatening the security of their sexual relationship, has been analysed as an example of Kubrick's use of contrasting acting styles for male and female characters. Prior to this confrontation, Tom Cruise plays Bill as a confident, successful, attractive, rather smug male, familiar from his repertoire of roles and his star persona. For Bingham, Cruise as Bill represents an Everyman; he appears to inhabit the role naturally and through his underplayed performance presents the character as a type rather than as possessing psychological complexity. The viewer is invited to think critically about the type and Cruise's personification of it, as he adopts a succession of masks in acting out his masculinity.[41] If Bill is almost a cypher, Kidman's Alice is 'Kubrick's most fully realized female character'. She is more physical and animated than her husband, conveying femininity through exaggerated gesture and changes of expression and demonstrating 'female character as postmodern pastiche'.[42]

During the confrontation, Kidman uses expressive techniques to transmit her anger while Cruise's face remains blank as though he is impervious to her provocation, which, as the subsequent scenes indicate, is not actually the case. This is one of several occasions in which the actors' features are compared to masks. At the end of the film, when Bill confesses his exploits to Alice, he breaks down in racking sobs as she cradles him in her arms on their bed. This is an unusual moment for Cruise and it is uncomfortable to watch and hear. He seems to be demonstrating the character's emotional collapse, especially as his face is positioned next to the mask he wore at the orgy. We do not see Alice's reaction at the time. The next day the couple sit in silence opposite one another, both weeping quietly. Bill's head is bowed; he does not meet his wife's gaze and covers his face with his hand. The camera lingers on Alice's tear-stained features as she attempts to contain her grief. Kidman's expression is mobile, communicating through a range of small inflections the signs of unhappiness. She sighs and swallows, looks at Bill and then looks down at her hand, which holds a cigarette, touching her thumb with her little finger in a nervous gesture before looking sideways and upwards and then back at Bill. Alice is the first to speak as she tells Bill that their daughter Helena expects them to take her Christmas shopping. Kidman speaks these apparently normal lines in a low, tremulous voice in between using facial expressions and hand

Tom Cruise and Nicole Kidman perform to
one another in *Eyes Wide Shut*

gestures to convey extreme emotional distress. Her accent, as in the rest of the film, is slightly contrived American with Australian undertones. Bill's stare in response is open to interpretation but it could indicate horror.

The players do not so much interact as perform to one another. The focus on Kidman's countenance and her expressive repertoire, played against Cruise's minimalist acting, reinforces the sense that the viewer is witnessing a charade. This perception is bolstered by the actors' stylised delivery of their lines in the final scene, where Alice takes the lead in their reconciliation. The couple seem to participate in a ritualistic exchange, displaying and questioning conventional gender roles. The dialogue, which has Alice reject the idea of permanent commitment, is eerily prescient of the impending Cruise/Kidman break-up. The film, in setting out to problematise the relationship between art and life, confirms that they are symbiotic, equally dependent on fabrication. Kubrick's didactic 'cinema of ideas', which drained both story and characters of emotion and identification, alienated many critics.[43] Cruise was deemed miscast and his monotone performance was compared negatively with Kidman's more nuanced and flamboyant turn as Alice. In a reversal of the usual dynamic governing their individual personas, Kidman's acting in *Eyes Wide Shut*, though extremely stylised, depicted Alice as a relatively rounded, authentic character in counterpoint to Cruise's flat portrayal of Bill.[44] Kidman's reputation as an actress benefited from the comparison, while Cruise's, rather unfairly, did not.[45]

Kidman's performance in *Eyes Wide Shut* was appreciated partly because it effectively channelled Kubrick's ideas but also because her deployment of expressive techniques was a source of dramatic interest in a film in which little happened.[46] In retrospect, it represented a turning point. Despite the fact that she had less screen time than Cruise, her range of skills was more in evidence than his. Her physical attributes were also on display, making her a source of visual fascination. Thus she successfully combined commodity stardom with a claim to acting talent. In the context of the film's play with illusion and reality, the artifice of her performance was appropriate and managed to conjure empathy even while it alienated. Authenticity resided primarily in the realisation of the director's vision but also in the actress's demonstrable ability to interpret it. The fact that Kidman's acting 'outshone' that of Cruise, perhaps to a degree that the director did not predict, not only made her a powerful heroine but conclusively emancipated her from her status as Mrs Tom Cruise. There was an excess in Kidman's performance that challenged Kubrick's patriarchal authority and that of her star husband. While this can be seen as apposite to the project and as an effect of film-making techniques, it also demonstrates that performance has a certain autonomy that can reach beyond the boundaries of the film text.

The Hours (Stephen Daldry, 2002)

The autonomy of screen performance operates on different levels. In its ostensive manifestations, it can work as a distraction from the narrative, inspiring aesthetic and moral debate about character motivation and appropriate behaviour, acting skills or personal characteristics.[47] It can trigger memories of other performances and acting traditions. Because it draws on public knowledge of the performer, it can affect perceptions of their persona. In institutional terms, it showcases the creative talent of individual actors bidding for industry recognition in the form of awards. In the competitive and uncertain climate of the contemporary star system, awards are important in enhancing an actor's reputation and in marketing films. The Academy Awards are the most prestigious and influential, promising peer esteem and increased public visibility combined with commercial benefits.[48] A nomination confers added value on an actor's performance, giving them creative capital that can be exchanged in negotiations on future projects. One nomination often leads to others, propelling the actor into a different league. The spectacular nature of awards ceremonies is an indication of their importance to the industry; the glamour and pageantry surrounding these events provide opportunities for self-validation and promotion across interconnected media forms directed at influencing consumer viewing habits. The high-profile and elaborate Academy Awards are also the most controversial, generating heated argument about ethnic, racial, age and gender bias and featuring melodramatic displays of emotion from the recipients. The 'red carpet' provides another performance space in which personal and professional dramas are played out and then recycled.

In 2002, Kidman received her first Best Actress Academy Award nomination for *Moulin Rouge!* (2001). *Moulin Rouge!* was nominated for eight awards and won Best Art Direction and Best Costume Design; though initial critical response was mixed, particularly in the US, the film went on to be a major hit. Kidman's rendition of the courtesan Satine projected her as an exotic diva, drawing on the iconography of classic Hollywood stars such as Marilyn Monroe, Rita Hayworth and Marlene Dietrich. While *Moulin Rouge!*'s irreverent take on the Hollywood musical was hardly conventional Oscar material, the fact that it was honoured in several categories helped to boost ancillary sales such as DVDs and contributed to its overall financial success. In Kidman's case, her nomination conferred industry recognition on her status as an actress following the perceived failure of *Eyes Wide Shut*. She also garnered praise and several award nominations for her performance as a psychologically unstable mother in Alejandro Amenábar's ghostly *The Others* (*Los otros*, 2001), which was a critical and box-office hit. With *The Hours*, scripted by David Hare from Michael Cunningham's Pulitzer Prize-winning novel exploring the lives of three unhappy women across different time periods, she launched a serious claim for an Academy Award in her role as iconic feminist writer Virginia

Nicole Kidman's Oscar-winning
transformation as Virginia Woolf in *The Hours*

Woolf. The project was supremely Oscar-worthy: a prestigious literary
adaptation featuring a score by Philip Glass and a line-up of respected
actors including Meryl Streep, Julianne Moore and Ed Harris, who
are art-house names rather than commodity stars. The choice of
Kidman to play Virginia Woolf was seen as controversial, partly
because she did not physically resemble the writer and partly because
her acting ability was deemed inadequate to the challenge.[49]

The film-makers justified their choice of Kidman by asserting
that they were intent on capturing the essence of Woolf rather than
striving for an accurate portrayal. Director Stephen Daldry admitted
the lack of physical resemblance but claimed to see in Kidman the
magnetism and sense of danger that characterised Woolf herself.
Considerable efforts were made to match Kidman's performance to
what was publicly known about Woolf, including fitting a prosthetic
nose. The left-handed actress learned to write with her right hand
and insisted on using it for the insert in which Woolf pens her suicide

note to her husband Leonard (Stephen Dillane). She also refused a stunt double for the drowning sequence that opens the film, which required her to be under water for long periods.[50] In interviews, Kidman emphasised the in-depth research she undertook to absorb the character, contending that her vulnerable emotional state following her divorce enabled her to tune into Woolf's depression. She played down the importance of the prosthetic nose, describing the role of make-up, costume and accessories in helping her to move and speak differently,[51] stating that smoking hand-rolled cigarettes as Woolf had done facilitated her transformation.[52] Her voice was significantly lowered and she adopted a clipped English accent that evoked rather than replicated Woolf's upper-middle-class tones.[53] Dialogue coach Sandra Frieze, who had worked on *Moulin Rouge!* and *The Others* and became Kidman's coach on *The Golden Compass* (2007) and *Australia* (2008), contributed to the vocal changes but the actress put them down entirely to her own efforts. Her willingness to abandon her glamorous star image in order to disguise herself as Woolf was praised by many critics.[54]

Kidman's physical transformation in *The Hours* was key to her bid for an Academy Award. Kevin Esch argues that 'actorly transformation' involving disciplined body alteration has become increasingly important in contemporary cinema in defining serious acting and conferring industry accolades on performers.[55] Actors are more likely to achieve award nominations if they display dedication to their craft by making themselves almost unrecognisable in portraying character. When an actor depicts a real person, their success is measured by the extent to which they efface their own appearance in the process; part of the transformation may be achieved by make-up and prosthetics but an arsenal of bodily modifications can be deployed, from weight loss or gain to stance and gesture. Esch traces the emergence of actorly transformation in the 1980s to a reformulation of 1950s Method concepts of 'becoming the part' whereby the actor based their performance on close observation of life and submerged themselves entirely in their subject.[56] However, Esch perhaps underestimates the extent to which the transformation itself is dramatised by the performance, allowing the actor's work (and by implication that of crew members such as make-up artists and voice coaches) to become visible. Displaying the craft involved in performance is important in the process of pitching for awards. At the same time, drawing attention to the actor's professional transformation skills endows them with gravitas and enables their identity to surface along with the character.

Kidman's portrayal of Virginia Woolf showcased her actorly transformation. She was deglamorised, her glossy mane hidden under an untidy dark wig and her body concealed by shapeless clothing. Make-up gave her skin a sallow appearance while the prosthetic nose elongated her features, altering her physiognomy and producing a melancholy expression. The nose added emphasis to her eyes, which were framed by unplucked eyebrows and were often narrowed into an angry stare. Her body movements and gestures were awkward and she slouched as she walked. Her voice was deep and cracked, while her English accent featured drawn-out vowel sounds and stressed consonants, delivering a contrived vocal performance that stood out from the more naturalistic style of the other players. One of her defining gestures as the heavy smoker Woolf was to brandish a hand-rolled cigarette as she talked – an image that was widely used in publicity material for the film. Despite the fact that *The Hours* was an ensemble piece built around strong performances from all the players, it was Kidman's impersonation of Virginia Woolf that took centre stage. Paradoxically her absorption into the character, which seemed to depend on making herself invisible, gave her more prominence. Rather than integrating the Woolf sections into the overall texture, Kidman's 'performance as performance' became the star turn that won her the Academy Award.

Kidman's commodity stardom was vital to the perception that her rendition of Woolf was the result of her acting talent and it gave her performance the edge over those of Julianne Moore and Meryl Streep, who were also nominated for leading actress awards.[57] The beauty and elegance of her star persona were in sharp contrast to the image of dishevelled self-neglect she projected as Woolf, which lent credence to the idea that she delved beneath the surface to make the writer's inner rage and unhappiness outwardly visible. Equally, the contrast ensured that Kidman's persona remained visible behind the character; for some, this meant that she had succeeded in establishing herself as a bona fide star.[58] However, not everyone responded positively to the interplay between Kidman's celebrity status and her actorly transformation. Wendy Parkins argues that the film's construction of an opposition between Kidman's beauty and Woolf's plainness aligns beauty with success and power and ugliness with failure and suffering. For Parkins, the prosthetic nose functions primarily as a signifier for Kidman's willingness to suffer for her art, thus obscuring the anguish of Woolf's struggle for creativity.[59] Parkins's focus on physical appearance tends to occlude the extent to which Kidman portrays Woolf as a star performer in her own right.[60] Her mannerisms do not just draw attention to her own performance, they also depict a melodramatic character aware of her audience whose life, work and death dramatised her rebellion against social norms. Kidman's actorly transformation produced a convergence between artistic genius and acting, elevating the status of her craft and signalling her own aspirations to greatness. The strategy paid off: with the critical and commercial success of *The Hours* and her Best Actress Academy Award, her career reached a peak.

Australia (Baz Luhrmann, 2008)

Dennis Bingham claims that Nicole Kidman 'demonstrates … female character as postmodern pastiche', citing a scene from *Moulin Rouge!*, in which she plays with different personas available to her in

Nicole Kidman's performance in *Moulin Rouge!*
opens up questions of identity

her seduction of the evil Duke.[61] He identifies Kidman's acting style with irony and display of actorly techniques directed at encouraging viewers to ponder questions of performance and femininity. Bingham implies that despite her emphasis on acting as masquerade, her deployment of pastiche offers authenticity because it opens up issues of gender identity. Kidman's acting is regularly associated with postmodernism, particularly in films that use pastiche to update source material, such as *Bewitched* (2005), a revival of the popular US television series, or *The Invasion* (2007), a modern adaptation of Jack Finney's 1955 sci-fi novel *The Body Snatchers*. But it is her collaboration with fellow Australian Baz Luhrmann that most clearly exemplifies her approach to postmodernist performance. Luhrmann's theatre and film work is characterised by collage, the juxtaposition of texts, images and styles from different periods to create imaginary fictional worlds that collapse time and place. It quotes liberally from world cinema and classic Hollywood, ostensibly as a form of homage; however, this activity frequently borders on travesty and can be seen as the appropriation and deconstruction of dominant cinematic tropes, emerging from his postcolonial Australian context.[62] Kidman's Australian background is key to her persona and her use of pastiche in performance can also be seen as postcolonial, highlighting questions of nationalism and identity in global culture. In the epic historical drama *Australia*, Luhrmann projects his country's history and identity as fragmentary and unsettled, constantly in the process of revision. Kidman's depiction of English aristocrat Lady Sarah Ashley, who undergoes a transformation through contact with Australian mores, draws on different types and techniques to complement this projection.

In his discussion of postmodernist performance in theatre, Philip Auslander refers to the 'death of character', outlining a move away from unified, psychologically consistent characters towards fractured personae who evade logical motivation and interpretation.[63] He takes as an example Jeffrey M. Jones's *Der Inka von Peru*, a play made up of texts appropriated from other sources in which the characters speak words that belong to others rather than to themselves or the play's author. Such characters do not represent coherent human beings with psychological depth but are themselves collages of texts drawn from various cultural contexts.[64] Auslander does not attribute political or counter-cultural value to this postmodernist device; however, such dislocated, culturally alienated characters can be seen to connect with the displaced figures of postcolonial drama. Postmodernism should not be equated with postcolonialism; Helen Gilbert and Joanne Tompkins argue that postcolonial theatre has a specific political agenda, to deconstruct and destabilise the power and authority of imperialism.[65] Nevertheless, postmodernist and postcolonial aesthetic strategies share common features. Although by Auslander's criteria, Luhrmann's work does not really qualify as postmodernist because character is anchored in story and theme, Luhrmann appropriates postmodernist tactics to denaturalise narrative conventions and disrupt audience expectations. In *Australia*, these methods are employed to disrupt dominant white European versions of national history, focusing on the controversial issue of the 'stolen generations', the mixed-race Aboriginal children who were removed from their families by the government to be brought up as white. In conception and execution, *Australia* conforms in many ways to the 'performance of history's unsettlement' that Joanne Tompkins describes as the motivating principle of postcolonial drama.[66]

Luhrmann's theatre training informs his anti-realist approach to acting, which draws on and quotes from different traditions. Characters in his films adopt histrionic modes of performance that often verge on the absurd. This estrangement technique produces mixed audience reactions from delight to derision and disgust. Kidman's non-naturalistic performance in *Australia* was widely criticised as bad acting, to the extent that Luhrmann was provoked to come to her defence.[67] It was, however, appreciated for its comic range and emotional authenticity by those more sympathetic to the film's agenda and aesthetic.[68] Lady Sarah's mutation from tightly wound English aristocrat to tomboy adventurer and romantic heroine is executed via multiple clashing storylines and genres and depends on a performance by Kidman that plays exaggerated styles, in which she appears to be acting in quotation marks, against a more naturalistic portrayal used in more intimate scenes. Her character is presented as a type, the effect of textual operations rather than a rounded individual but, because this method is tied to naturalistic performance intended to provide an emotional connection for viewers, it is not strictly postmodernist. Sometimes the technique is used to induce an emotional response, as in the scene in which Lady Sarah awkwardly relates 'The Wizard of Oz' to the recently bereaved Nullah, the Aboriginal boy at the centre of the story. Kidman's acting is characterised by artifice; her costume is close-fitting and her hair is pinned back, visualising her buttoned-up Englishness, while her British accent and diction appear contrived. Her features and gestures are mobile, emphasising physical expression. Her lines are delivered with numerous hesitations and vocal mannerisms and she frequently moves her head to avoid eye contact with Nullah. Brandon Walters, on the other hand, depicts Nullah in naturalistic terms as an authentic character. However, because the scene is built around cultural exchange and language, no simple opposition between artifice and authenticity is made and an emotional rapport between Lady Sarah and Nullah is established.

In this scene and elsewhere, there are elements of mimicry in Kidman's performance. The comic sequence in which Lady Sarah journeys with the rugged Drover (Hugh Jackman) across the Australian desert to the Faraway Downs homestead pivots on a conflict between Lady Sarah's upper-class sense of moral superiority and the Drover's rough-and-ready contempt for manners. Their prickly relationship deliberately echoes that between Katharine Hepburn and Humphrey Bogart in *The African Queen* (1951) and

Caricature: Nicole Kidman's hyperbolic
performance in *Australia*

Kidman's body language, vocal delivery and comedy techniques
imitate Hepburn's, often using broad, cartoon-like forms of
expression. *Australia* is laden with quotations from Hollywood
movies; Luhrmann's habit of borrowing from other cinematic
sources is sometimes described as his way of paying tribute to them.
However, the hyperbolic excess and overtones of caricature through
which such appropriations are re-presented suggest ambivalence
rather than homage. Kidman's use of mimicry is not that described
by postcolonial theorists as the colonised's resistance to their
disempowerment and she is not the silenced subject envisaged by
such theory.[69] Indeed, her whiteness is a feature of her persona.[70]
Nevertheless, her imitation as an Australian actress of classical
Hollywood performance renders the language of dominant cinema as
cliché, opening up a space in which the desire for alternative story-
telling modes and identities can be intimated, though not realised.
The act of mimicry simultaneously dramatises the postcolonial
impulse to sweep away the stifling traditions of official culture and
the difficulty of producing new and original forms under its sway. In

its emphasis on repetition, mimicry produces characters who are cyphers at the service of others and whose agency is limited.

Sharon Marie Carnicke points out that all actors employ different styles and techniques and their choices depend on context.[71] It is true that Kidman's work is not universally characterised by overt mimicry and the adoption of masks. In films such as *Margot at the Wedding* (2007) or *Rabbit Hole* (2010), her portrayals are delivered in broadly naturalistic modes appropriate to the projects. Even so, as an actress and star her style and persona can be described as 'actorly', defined by the self-conscious display of skills and occupation of different types rather than the projection of a unified, coherent character. As noted, this trait alienates those who prefer naturalism but it can also be a source of fascination and inspire admiration for her talent. Kidman's actorly identity performs several functions: by highlighting her artistic credentials, it provides an additional, contradictory, dimension to her commodity stardom, enabling her to cross over between art and popular cinema; it draws attention to her aspiration to serious actress status; and it is directed at achieving industry recognition and accumulating creative capital in the form of major awards. As the above discussion indicates, it also has other, less calculated ramifications to do with her position as an Australian woman working in the contemporary global entertainment industries. By looking at Kidman's performances over a range of titles and periods, it is possible to see not only her development as an actress/star but also her cultural significance in international cinema, achieved despite career vagaries.

* * *

It is virtually impossible to describe the details of on-screen performance without ascribing agency and intention to the actor. This is the case even though film acting is mediated by technological and other factors that interact to produce what appears on the screen. The actor's work and deployment of skills, their creative input and reinterpretation of character, operate together with these factors before, during and after shooting rather than being directly reproduced or recorded. Although this may seem an obvious point, conceptions of screen acting cling to the idea that the film actor's body and voice exist, as Pamela Robertson Wojcik puts it, apart from the cinematic.[72] Screen performance clearly differs from theatre, in which the actor is present on stage – though even here the performance is not free from technological and other forms of intervention.[73] Nevertheless, approaches to film acting generally assume the presence of the actor and attribute the source of the performance to their unique deployment of skills. Wojcik and other scholars point out that the specifics of cinematic performance allow us to think about film acting differently, without assuming that it derives from a pre-existing source or directly from the actor's identity. While this appears to downgrade the participation of actors, it brings to the fore the collaborative nature of film-making in addition to challenging the realist notion that in film performance the actor's body, gestures and voice express the interior emotional state of the character.[74]

Kidman's acting style, with its emphasis on artifice and pastiche, draws attention to performance as surface rather than the expression of inner psychological depth, even though the latter is the focus of much of the discourse that surrounds her work. Despite attempts to match her acting skills and intention with character and the search for authenticity and realism in interviews and other promotional materials, her gestural and vocal performance on screen tends to highlight technological factors such as make-up and hair, costume, lighting, music, sound and colour. Dennis Bingham compares Kidman's histrionic turn in *Moulin Rouge!* to 'items on an epicurean Delsartean menu after 150 years of sampling', referring to the lexicon of vocal and bodily gestures compiled by influential nineteenth-century French acting teacher François Delsarte.[75] Through her cartoonish exhibition of technique Kidman mocks and exposes the limited array of feminine types available to her and draws attention to their roots in acting traditions. Her display also brings to mind the graphic illustrations used by Delsarte and others to depict the repertoire of actors' posture and gesture.[76] In the age of digital technologies when the actor's physical presence is ever further removed from their on-screen manifestation, film performance may have more affinity with animation.[77] Without denying star agency, in analysing the details of physiognomic, vocal and bodily expression it seems appropriate to turn to the reality of cinema rather than to the actor's corporeal existence for the realisation of character. Although Kidman's performance style combines naturalistic and ostensive traditions, in its propensity for demonstration of technique, it facilitates this shift in perception.

3 PERSONA

The performance of celebrity

The public persona is the linchpin that holds together aspects of the star identity and activity spanning diverse locations and forms. It is a slippery entity consisting of relatively stable core features such as name and basic life story that intersect with more unpredictable time- and context-sensitive elements that produce celebrity fame. The persona is a fiction, as much a character as any dramatic role and as reliant on acting ability, even when the star is not physically present. According to Barry King, it brings together the so-called private person and the parts they play in films to create a type capable of satisfying market-led rather than artistic imperatives.[1] King contends that in the contemporary global industry, with its multiplying commercial spin-offs, product sponsorship, promotion and advertising deals have as much significance as indicators of value as the star's critical reception and box-office success, while their performances extend into spheres such as music, theatre and television. In these circumstances, the star's reputation rests on a portfolio of performance expertise rather than on their accomplishments in film and skills of self-presentation, acquired through training, are equally if not more important than those of character acting.[2] The modern star celebrity (as opposed to a character actor, though they may be both) operates between film and extra-cinematic appearances to achieve maximum publicity, becoming a personal brand. They may still privilege the cinematic execution of their craft as part of their self-presentation, which enables the persona to retain artistic credibility that can then be exchanged. Nicole Kidman's commodity stardom epitomises the construction of a multifaceted identity or brand that is fundamental to the employment practices of today's entertainment industries, where visibility influences perceptions of market value. It also has symbolic and cultural aspects, presented through narrative and other forms of representation.

Celebrity performance is usually placed on the side of entertainment rather than art and is regarded as motivated by vested corporate interests as well as those of stars themselves.[3] Comparatively little attention has been paid to the details of celebrity performance skills or to the conventions of the modes in which they appear. In this chapter, I explore some of the arenas in which Kidman's fame is produced, enacted, managed and exploited before discussing the significance of her Australian identity in stabilising her persona. Although celebrity construction and performance are primarily tied to marketing and self-promotion, it is misleading to use the opposition between art and commerce to differentiate the craft of cinematic acting from extra-cinematic celebrity activity. In the first place, they are intimately connected and in the second, the products of cinema, whatever their claims to artistry, are commodities produced by businesses dedicated to making profit. The recognition that 'cinema' covers an increasingly wide range of media enterprises is justification enough for taking all these interrelated operations seriously as cultural events. As with film acting, it is important to dislodge preconceptions that celebrity performance originates in the body and intentions of the star. Even live appearances, where both celebrity and audience are palpably present, are rehearsed, governed by formal conventions, produced by specific technologies and disseminated to other audiences across

Nicole Kidman thanks her fans via her YouTube channel

media outlets that have their own aesthetic protocols. Equally, though the star may appear to be in charge of the construction of their image, their participation is carried out intermittently at different stages in collaboration with a number of creative, business and technical personnel and their say over how the image is used in parts of the media is circumscribed.

The star celebrity is projected as a special individual via myriad channels. The press, leisure and lifestyle magazines, book publishing, photo shoots, radio and television appearances, award ceremonies, film festivals, philanthropic functions, advertising, online databases, websites, Wikipedia, YouTube and the internet contribute to the circulation of information and meaning by relaying and replaying highly conventionalised stories and visual representations. Performances in film and television cameos, music videos, commercials and DVD extra materials also play a part in establishing star identity. Although star discourse has always been distributed across different media, the proliferation of electronic communication channels and the networks that connect them has both increased the amount of information that is generated and opened up more direct forms of access. Opportunities for unauthorised interaction with the process of constructing celebrity stardom have mushroomed, making the gossip circuit a more powerful conduit for speculation and alternative versions of official star narratives. Conversations formerly confined to private enclaves are now made public via online discussion boards. In this situation, control of the circulation of star images exercised by studios, publicity agents and stars themselves has dissipated and personas have fragmented. As contradictory views vie with one another the sense of a 'real', unique and coherent self behind the star persona has given way to a more fluid and contested notion of identity. King argues that this decentred, labile construction of fame exists because it is commercially efficacious;[4] however, it has other dimensions. The input of diverse agencies with different kinds and degrees of investment creates a culture of dispute and dialogue in which, although hierarchies are in operation, power relations are less settled.

Privacy laws

One area in which this is evident is that of celebrity rights to privacy and publicity. Outlining the legal measures that regulate celebrity image ownership, Philip Drake maintains that the court appearances through which stars assert ownership and claim compensation from those who intrude on their privacy contribute to the circulation of star discourse by producing dramatic scenarios of celebrity and power.[5] In 2003, Kidman won substantial undisclosed damages in the UK courts against the *Daily Mail* and *Sun* newspapers, who reported that she had an affair with her *Cold Mountain* (2003) co-star Jude Law that led to the break-up of his marriage to Sadie Frost.[6] Kidman asserted that the story caused her personal and professional damage, particularly as it coincided with the run-up to the 2003 Academy Awards, where she was nominated as Best Actress for *The Hours* (2002).[7] Kidman was not present for the hearing but the story was widely circulated in the media; in interviews, when asked why she responded to this rumour as opposed to others she gave as reasons the fact that Law was married with children and the need to protect her own children from scandal.[8] Ostensibly, the lawsuit was not about money, since Kidman donated the damages to a Romanian orphanage (which allowed her to acquire other kinds of capital). Rather it dramatised a struggle over ownership in which Kidman regained control of her image, asserting her authority at a time when her career and profile were reaching a peak. The case, which she would not have undertaken without considering the consequences, gained her additional attention in her bid to consolidate her star power. It also generated a story in which the star's relationship with her audiences was tested and the limits of consumer rights to freedom of expression were highlighted. Drake points out that privacy legislation has played a part in defining the extent of celebrity power.[9] Court action provides a public arena in which the dynamic between star and consumer is played out.

Despite the fact that Kidman was not present at the hearing, the legal proceedings can be seen as a performance. Kidman was the protagonist in a narrative focusing on a quest for truth and justice in which an individual was pitted against a formidable corporate adversary. In interviews she used self-presentation skills to portray her motivations as morally responsible, projecting a heroic persona. At the same time the case opened up a dialogue between the star and consumers, on one hand asserting her right to privacy, on the other courting attention and inviting a response. This tension between individual freedom and the public's right to know is at the heart of celebrity culture and can be seen in more playful kinds of dialogue that take place between stars and the media. Speculation about Kidman's fertility was rife from the early days of her marriage to Tom Cruise and intensified after the couple adopted their children Isabella and Connor. When she married Keith Urban in 2006, a wave of pregnancy rumours circulated in the tabloids and celebrity press; following the birth of their daughter Sunday Rose in 2008, further conjecture ensued that she may be pregnant again. These stories were accompanied by candid photographs of the actress apparently displaying a 'baby bump'.[10] Photographs of Kidman at a music awards ceremony in 2009 showing her looking directly into camera, one hand cradling her stomach and a finger held to her lips as though she had a secret, caused widespread excitement in the press, although assumptions that this confirmed her pregnancy turned out to be false.[11] With this piece of play-acting, Kidman deliberately toyed with media intrusion into her personal life in order to ferment and frustrate the rumour mill. It was simultaneously a calculated bid for exposure, a commentary on invasion of privacy and an assertion that she had privileged access to the truth.

Television talk shows

The play with notions of star power in celebrity performance extends to other areas of public appearance such as television. P. David Marshall sets out the different ways in which film and television position their celebrities, with film stardom defined by an aura of distinction and television personalities by familiarity.[12] Discussing the specific format and performance conventions of talk shows, he outlines the role of the host in bringing film stars from the rarefied ambience of their movie roles into the realms of the everyday and the use of humour in getting the star to reveal details about their private lives, a process that plays on the tension between ordinariness and special qualities in star personas. For Marshall, television talk-show hosts participate in the construction of stardom by aiding the creation of a character or persona for the star. While the host has an identity, they gain celebrity status through proximity to other celebrities.[13] In 2004, Kidman appeared on *The Ellen DeGeneres Show* (2003–) as part of the promotion drive for *Birth* (2004).[14] The live interview was preceded by a teaser in which host DeGeneres is in the middle of a frantic telephone call trying to find a big star guest for

Ellen DeGeneres brings Nicole
Kidman down to earth

the show when Kidman knocks on her dressing-room door wanting
to hang out because her car has broken down.[15] The distracted
DeGeneres tries to get rid of her then, realising her mistake,
persuades the hesitant Kidman to appear as one of her guests,
offering to lend her some of her own clothes. The teaser plays on the
exceptional nature of Kidman's star glamour in contrast to the
dressed-down DeGeneres's informal presentation style. The elegance
of Kidman's clothing, jewellery, make-up and glossy, long blonde
hair give her a look of carefully designed untidiness that appears
exotic against DeGeneres's ordinariness, which seems natural. Her
sultry voice and Australian accent also mark her as special, while
Degeneres's vocal style is familiar from her comic persona. Both
celebrities are acting but each uses different conventions deriving
from their professional contexts to project a distinctive persona. This
produces an ironic commentary on the relationship between film
stardom and television celebrity that the interview reinforces.

In the teaser, DeGeneres acts as the conduit for Kidman's
journey from the rarefied world of movie glamour to television's
staging of the everyday. During the interview that follows, the
contrast in their visual styles and body language remains marked,
with Kidman sitting upright with her knees together while

DeGeneres's stance is more casual, as she rests her hand on her right leg, which is balanced on her left knee.[16] The set, which has a fire in the background, resembles a living room. Kidman appears relaxed and laughs a lot, responding to the studio audience as well as to the host, which increases the atmosphere of intimacy and accessibility. DeGeneres begins with questions about her film career and moves on to more personal territory with her predilection for extreme sports. When DeGeneres asks about her children, Kidman hesitates and appears resistant to saying too much. In a comic reference to the contrived familiarity of the setting and to invasion of privacy, DeGeneres pretends to pick up the phone to call Isabella. When Kidman's hair falling on her lapel microphone causes a sound blip, DeGeneres uses the occurrence to make fun of the star's super-glamorous locks, highlighting the fact that her style is out of place in the homely surroundings. Kidman regains the ground of ordinariness by referring to her habit of honking when she laughs, whereupon DeGeneres suggests car bumper stickers bearing the legend 'Honk if you love Nicole', reducing her star aura to the level of the banal. Kidman appears to enjoy the joke but when DeGeneres returns to the subject of her children, she forcefully reasserts her power by making it clear that she will not answer any more questions about them. Later, DeGeneres refers to Kidman's skill with different accents, joking about her own lack of acting ability. In this exchange, artifice is associated with film and non-acting with television. When the host displays a two-page magazine spread featuring the Chanel No. 5 advertising campaign and mentions the Baz Luhrmann commercial, Kidman professes to be embarrassed at being confronted with her professional persona in the personal context of the interview. DeGeneres underscores this when she again emphasises the difference between them by claiming that she is available to appear in perfume commercials herself.

The interview exemplifies the ambivalence and synergies that exist between the media and celebrity stardom. DeGeneres mocks

Staging the everyday:
Nicole Kidman on *The Ellen
DeGeneres Show*

Kidman's star persona and power at the same time as promoting it
by encouraging her to reveal her more private side. She uses humour
to put Kidman at a disadvantage; although the actress is skilful at
recovery, she appears taken by surprise and therefore more human at
times. DeGeneres adopts a contradictory attitude that is reverent
towards Kidman's acting talent yet sets out to cut her movie-star
aura down to size. Her own persona connotes lack of star quality,
concealing her status as a powerful celebrity performer. In the
exchanges between the two women, which pivot on a contrast
between public persona and private self, the conventions of television
realism are revealed. The set-up and performances are as staged as
any in film or theatre; although parts of the conversation seem
impromptu, there is clearly a rudimentary script and it is likely that
Kidman and her 'people' met with the show's producers and host to
discuss what would (and could) be covered. DeGeneres represents
the audience's conflicting feelings towards powerful stars: the desire
to get close to those who are worshipped from afar and expose them.
These mixed emotions have a further dimension; in playing off
Kidman's artificiality against DeGeneres's naturalism, an opposition
is created between the star's carefully styled heterosexual image,
designed to be looked at, and the rumpled refusal of fashion
characteristic of DeGeneres's gay identity. In the context of the show,

this contrast of styles both hints at the rumours surrounding Kidman's (hetero)sexuality and confirms DeGeneres's sexuality as more authentic. The visual aspects of the performance and setting contribute an allusive subtext to the interview that plays on known elements of Kidman's public persona without directly referring to them. Whether she is aware of this is not entirely clear.

Magazine fashion shoots

Kidman's elegance and status as a fashion icon are central to her commodity stardom and her projection of herself as a brand. Although this aspect circulates across media outlets, the strongest focus on her star glamour occurs in high-end fashion and lifestyle magazines such as *Vanity Fair*, *Vogue* and *Harper's Bazaar*, which are directed at consumers interested in culture, politics and style. Kidman's exposure in these magazines is extensive, even excessive; her tall, slim physique is eminently suited to displaying designer clothing while her investment in beauty makes her supremely photogenic. In addition, fashion's predilection for performance, masquerade and mutable identities makes it the ideal theatre for presenting her multifaceted persona and acting ability. The coverage is conventionalised; it consists of photo-shoot images supported by a feature, generally containing interview material with the star and those who know her, that recycles well-known details from Kidman's biography, combined with updated information about her current and future film work. The style and tone of the articles are complimentary even when touching on difficult or controversial personal issues. Almost without exception, they present the star in a positive light, although in some cases the persona projected by the photo shoot contrasts with that presented by the article.[17] The feature articles set out a familiar story focused on life events while the photo-shoot images are removed from the everyday, depicting her as an idealised figure. Although there are elements of fantasy in both articles and photo shoots, it is more strongly marked in the images, where she adopts an assortment of guises around which readers may weave their own daydreams.

The fashion shoots feature a cover picture of Kidman, linked to the images inside the magazine, in which she appears in a frontal pose directed at the viewer. The cover shot and byline entice consumers to buy the magazine in order to enjoy looking at the star and to possess her image. The illusion of access to inside knowledge and possession of Kidman's image promised by such coverage sells magazines and is a primary mechanism for acquiring maximum public attention for the star. Some of the covers are racy, implying intimacy with the viewer and playing on their sexual fantasies.[18] In his biography of Kidman, David Thomson describes a glamour shoot for the December 2004 issue of Italian *GQ* displaying a seductive cover portrait of the star for a special feature on the world's 100 most beautiful women, in which she came top. As he points out, her victory was an editorial decision and it is likely that there were business negotiations involved in the nature of her participation, which she did not have to accept. Thomson is both titillated by the photos in the eight-page spread devoted to Kidman and surprised that the actress who played Virginia Woolf in *The Hours* was prepared to portray herself as a 'sex kitten' and to allow *GQ* to include two pages of nude shots from her movies.[19] He wonders whether she agreed to the spread or whether she regards such exploitation as part of the package. He is provoked to question Kidman's financial and professional power, which he assumes would allow her to dictate the terms of her engagement in such publicity stunts. Thomson's discussion reveals the complex interaction between commodity stars and consumers, which is characterised by mixed reactions, moral judgment and contestation. It also points up the difficulties many critics and academics have in reconciling artistic achievement with commerce-driven work in stars' activities despite the general understanding that they are both important to the job.

Fashion's brightest star:
Nicole Kidman in *Vogue* photo
shoot (*Vogue*, September 2003,
photograph: Annie Leibovitz)

As with Kidman's movie appearances, her performance in
fashion shoots involves the input of teams of creative, business and
technical personnel, some of whom are credited on the photographs.
Just as the promotion of a film often features the name of an
auteur, the quality fashion shoot gives prominence to renowned
photographers, designers and brand names. Despite their
commercial motivations, a high level of artistry, craft and theatrical
display is apparent in the shoots. Although the photographs are not
scripted in the conventional sense, they depict Kidman as characters
in stories consumers can develop for themselves. The characters
and style of the photos vary with the photographer in the same
way that the director influences the look of a film and the actors'
performances. The photo-shoots are tied into and draw on the star's
film work. In September 2003, when Kidman's success was at a peak
following her Best Actress Academy Award for *The Hours*, *Vogue*
magazine featured a lavish twenty-page spread of portraits of her by
top photographers Irving Penn, Annie Leibovitz, Helmut Newton
and Craig McDean supported by a short feature article.[20] The
magazine cover displays a Leibovitz shot of a divaesque Kidman
standing on a gleaming stage, lit from behind by theatre spotlights,
looking directly at the camera with a steady, almost challenging gaze.
Her height is emphasised by her hairstyle, which is swept upward,
and by her revealing dress, which is transparent and skin-tight with a

voluminous train. Her head and shoulders break into the *Vogue* masthead and a headline proclaims: 'Fashion's brightest star: Nicole Kidman on life as an icon'. On the contents page, a box entitled 'Cover look: Venus rising' lists credits for the dress (Atelier Versace mermaid gown), jewellery, make-up, hair, photographer and fashion editor.

Leibovitz's cover shot, in which Kidman's body is clearly photographically enhanced, is artistic at the same time as projecting an eroticised vision of the star that emphasises her physical allure and elegance as sources of power. A letter from the editor pays tribute to the influence of Kidman's 'polish and innate sense of chic' on the fashion world's understanding of glamour, referring to her as an icon.[21] The spread opens with a double-page monochrome head-and-shoulders shot by Irving Penn in which she appears pensive and a little melancholy, gazing off-camera with her head tilted to the side and her hand held up to her chin and mouth. The lighting and Kidman's dress and hairstyle give the photo an arty retro look, also evident in Penn's other monochrome shot of the star in a Rochas tiered brocade gown, where she sports a parasol. A box with credits for the dress, jewellery, hair and make-up features a quote from the designer Olivier Theyskens: 'Nicole is always Nicole, no matter who made the dress', confirming Kidman's star status in the fashion world. These sentiments are echoed in the feature article, which is littered with quotations from the likes of John Galliano, Valentino and Tom Ford, extolling her beauty and sense of style. A distinction is made between her red-carpet appearances, where she is always herself, and her performances in film, where she becomes someone else. In upcoming films such as *The Human Stain* (2003), *Cold Mountain* and *Birth* she is 'arguably the most versatile and consistently surprising actress of her generation ... and she is fearless in pursuit of her craft'.[22] 'Being herself' does not mean revealing the 'real' Nicole Kidman; rather, as Tom Ford puts it, 'She's developed a character for the red carpet, a public persona that is very groomed, very sleek, very controlled ... very much the star ...'. According to Emanuel Ungaro, 'Nobody seems to really know Nicole Kidman because she has pulled off the miracle of being recognized in her art without unveiling herself', while Craig McDean is quoted as saying 'I don't think she likes looking natural.' The article goes on to claim that Kidman has achieved iconicity by adopting a variety of looks and masks. Baz Luhrmann acknowledges that the red carpet is part of her job, 'and, boy, is it a lot of work'.[23]

The article foregrounds the connections between Kidman's fashion and film performance, seeing them both as the result of artistic endeavour, hard work and professionalism. In between the accolades, it offers astute commentary on the nature of Kidman's stardom and the construction of her persona. Kidman is presented as a lead character, supported by a cohort of top creative talent, in the story of her own success. The extent of her achievement can be measured by the amount of space devoted to her, the tributes paid by so many leading fashion names and the high production values of the photo shoot. The article's affirmation of Kidman's persona as a collection of different guises is supported by the photo shoot which, in addition to the Irving Penn shots, depicts her in tomboy mode, androgynous in fashionable menswear and displaying attitude (Craig McDean); as the height of exclusive glamour in *haute couture* (Annie Leibovitz); and as sultry sex goddess in revealing underwear (Helmut Newton). A supplementary array of images under the title 'Getting It Right' celebrates her skill at choosing the right outfit for every occasion. Kidman's performance on the red carpet and in fashion shoots is not regarded as subsidiary; it is given equivalent status with her film work, and both are considered equally important to her persona. The *Vogue* feature constructs her star identity and defines the source of her power, illuminating the extent of her investment in the image and its significance for modern commodity stardom.

Celebrity tabloid gossip

Whereas the quality lifestyle magazines focus respectfully on positive aspects of Kidman's life and work, devising a heroic character, the celebrity press does the obverse. Concentrating on secrets, scandal and speculation, the celebrity tabloids set out to expose what lies beneath the surface of the star image. In the case of female celebrities, the attention paid to their bodies, appearance, dress, family and emotional tribulations is relentless. The coverage is ephemeral and has the immediacy of gossip, returning constantly to the same themes. In Kidman's case, these revolve around rumours about her sex life and sexuality, marriage, children, fertility and plastic surgery, and commentary on her image, finances, work and sartorial style. Because of the emphasis on the exposé, invasion of privacy is a major issue and Kidman has on occasion asserted her rights in this respect.[24] The circulation of star discourse in the tabloid press may seem to be less top-down than in quality magazines and television talk shows, outside the control of the star and her publicity agencies. The activity of constructing and deconstructing the star image and persona via rumour mills appears to be the province of consumers. However, although the star celebrity may have substantial input in their appearances in more upscale media, as my discussion above demonstrates, there are limits to their power over editorial decisions there too. When it comes to the tabloids, coverage is defined by to-and-fro between rumour and denial, all of which contribute to building character and story. Such exchanges are part and parcel of the interdependent relationship between famous personalities and the media in the pursuit of public interest.

As a powerful star celebrity, Kidman is on show all the time. Even seemingly private moments are captured by candid photographs that apparently catch her unawares.[25] These off-the-record glimpses give the illusion that the consumer is privy to inside information that the star would prefer not to make public. In contrast to her appearances on the red carpet, in fashion magazines and on television where her awareness of the camera is part of the performance, in candid shots she often behaves as though she is off camera even when she knows that photographers are present. She colludes with the processes of celebrity exposure up to a point while resisting intrusion into her privacy in certain areas. After the birth of her first daughter, when she was forty-one, Kidman nurtured rumours that she may be pregnant again by stating in interviews that she would like another child with Keith Urban. In 2010, stories circulated that the couple were undergoing fertility treatment, with Kidman's age a key issue, and she was reported to be on 'celebrity bump watch'.[26] Her body was subjected to a frenzy of inspection; candid photographs of her exposed stomach appeared in the tabloid press, fuelling speculation,[27] while Kidman's denials only intensified the rumours.[28] In January 2011, she and Urban announced the birth of their second daughter via 'gestational carrier', a controversial term that generated debate in the press, already fired up over the couple's decision to use surrogacy and their success at keeping the birth secret.[29] The story was not a scandal – the use of surrogates by celebrities has become more common in recent years – but the assertion of the right to secrecy by Kidman was a challenge to the power of the media and set limits on the public's right to know. The revelation had the effect of precipitating a spate of media comment, further boosting Kidman's profile.

Kidman is adept at playing the rumour, denial and disclosure game. When celebrities issue denials, they are generally assumed to be hiding something, which exacerbates speculation. Revelations then acquire additional impact. Kidman's commodity stardom depends on the photogenic appeal of her face and body; just as her appearance in films is crafted using cosmetics and prosthetics, her public image is designed and created by teams of stylists and hair and make-up technicians. However, while disguise is regarded as laudable in the execution of her art, it is deemed deceitful when it comes to her off-screen image. Her assumed use of skin and body enhancement techniques such as Botox and plastic surgery are presented as revealing her beauty as fake, with a consequent loss of authenticity and esteem.[30] It is accepted by the tabloid press that celebrities work on their image as part of their job; considerable space is devoted to discussion of stars' fitness regimes, weight loss and gain and other physical changes. But the obsessive appraisal and critique of female celebrities' appearance betrays complex emotions, including fascination with and distrust of images, an impossible desire for intimate contact with famous personalities and the impulse to demean the rich and powerful. Personalities and tabloids alike exploit these feelings to keep consumer interest alive. Attempts to fend off the effects of ageing are a particular preoccupation, providing material for dramas of personal and professional success and failure through before-and-after and surgical disaster scenarios.[31]

Kidman's reputed fondness for Botox, which she consistently denied despite visible evidence of lip enhancement and other procedures, led to reports that her acting had suffered and a spate of jokes at the expense of her forehead.[32] Botox is controversial for health and other reasons; it works by freezing the face muscles.[33] As its widespread use as an anti-ageing treatment by A-list stars became a discussion topic, the stigma attached to it developed into a debate about the pressures on stars to remain looking young.[34] Comments from casting agents and directors such as Baz Luhrmann and Martin Scorsese about the difficulty of finding actresses with expressive features contributed to a growing antipathy towards the use of Botox and admissions by female stars that they had used it.[35] The fact that digital and HD technologies reveal fine details of the face and body, so that the evidence of augmentation is discernible, was a contributing factor. This context led to Kidman's confession in 2010 that she had used Botox but had now stopped.[36] She claimed to have retrieved her demonstrative forehead. Kidman's revelation went against her previous disclaimers; this was clearly less important than drawing attention to her renewed acting prowess or achieving publicity. It also served the purpose of explaining why her face had become perceptibly Botox-free, probably for health reasons connected to her first pregnancy and fertility treatment. The arguments around and backlash against Botox in the industry resulted in a cultural shift in which leading actresses, including Kidman, proclaimed their intention to remain 'natural' and renounce cosmetic procedures.[37] A characteristic scepticism about such claims was evident in parts of the celebrity press.[38]

Botox and other measures are part of Kidman's effort to create a personal brand, a proprietary image that caters to preconceptions of beauty and can be exchanged in the marketplace. When the use of Botox became detrimental to the brand, she overhauled her public image, adopting a curly red hairstyle reminiscent of her youth. Just as Botox eradicates the marks of time on the human face, Kidman's 'natural' re-brand, by returning to her younger incarnation, symbolised her determination to defy the ageing process and remained consistent with the tenets of the glamour industry. The Botox story touches on a number of cultural issues, including social ideals of beauty; female sexuality and ageing; technology and naturalism; the desire to control time; the search for reality; and loss of identity.[39] Botox's creation of frozen faces free from the signs of lived experience generates masks that expunge the existence of the individual human being and personal history assumed to lie behind the image. Kidman's use and rejection of Botox and her assumption of a natural guise epitomise the performance of her star persona as pure façade without an authentic self. In its drive to strip away the masquerade, the celebrity tabloid press contributes to the exposure and deconstruction of the processes of commodity stardom even as it shores them up.

Fan websites

In his study of online manifestations of stardom, Paul McDonald claims that the increasing presence of star discourse on the internet has facilitated the expansion of fan communities and more wide-ranging forms of interactive engagement with star images.[40] Official and fan websites represent a small but important part of the complex interaction between stars and fans. While official sites promote the star by purporting to speak on their behalf, fan sites do so through a discourse of personal adulation. They are usually individually authored, though they include forums and discussion boards through which fans exchange information, opinions and collected materials. These materials range from scans of magazine photo shoots and press articles to video and sound clips, photographs and press releases. In recent years, fan sites have become more technically sophisticated and professional, displaying high-quality images and video, attracting advertising and asking for donations. Links via Twitter and Facebook enhance the possibilities for fast circulation of news and information to wider fan communities. The home page of *Nicole's Magic*, which claims to be the No. 1 Kidman fan site, hosts a multitude of attractions from current projects and latest photos, news updates and featured movie to a sidebar displaying a link to Kidman's official site, and latest tweets, to a featured photograph, a link to the official *Rabbit Hole* (2010) website and a special project dedicated to celebrating Kidman's birthday.[41]

Menus offer access to everything available about the star, including news archives, song lyrics, a library of article transcripts, biography and filmography. A gallery of more than 3,000 photograph albums, organised under categories, covers her film, television, stage and music performances, her appearances on the red carpet, photo shoots, charitable work and candid shots. A media section offers wallpapers, stationery, banners, avatars and art by fans. A page for interaction includes Kidman-related games, merchandise and

Quality production: Nicole Kidman fan site
Nicole's Magic

opportunities to express opinions on the star's work and appearance. Another page features her style and fashion leadership, covering clothes, hair and make-up, body and fitness regimes. On the links page, fans can consult and add their names to Kidman fan listings and check out affiliated sites while the forum page allows them to post comments in eight categories. The design and production values of *Nicole's Magic* are high quality and it is easy to navigate, which increases its authority as a primary source of information about the star. It is driven not only by devotion to its subject but also by the desire to produce a comprehensive database of information capable of satisfying the demand for knowledge about the star from other fans.

The urge to 'know' the star is a primary motivation for fans and triggers the impulse to collect merchandise, memorabilia and materials relating to them. This is not so different from the completism that inspires the archivist. *Nicole's Magic* organises its information methodically into themed categories rather like a library collection. Although the information is gathered from sources of variable reliability, the scans of magazine and press articles, photos, screen caps, video and sound clips represent an unofficial archive offering items that may not be readily available elsewhere. Books and academic articles about Kidman are not listed; the emphasis is on ephemeral data that would otherwise be lost. The effect is to produce a record of the star's life and work constructed by fans that acts as a memory bank. The memories are accessed and reordered through interactive processes, much like a scrapbook or photograph album. McDonald disputes the commonly held view of fans as alienated individuals and also queries recent conceptions of fan communities as creating oppositional cultures, arguing that it is difficult to distinguish online fan writing from film-marketing discourse.[42] However, the role of the fan as archivist has perhaps been neglected. The tone of fan websites is celebratory and they are supportive of the star brand. Nevertheless, the scattered fragments of the star persona they bring together provide opportunities for recombination rather than a unified whole. While these online collections of materials about stars are not counter-cultural in themselves, the forms of knowledge they recycle can be put to any number of uses.

Commercials

In addition to selling films, the commodity star undertakes a range of marketing activities including sponsorship, advertising and product endorsements. While this has always been the case, the increased emphasis on branding and the expansion of cross-media networks in the contemporary entertainment industries have resulted in the growth and realignment of publicity operations. A star's involvement in an advertising campaign now extends across multiple outlets such as the press, magazines, film, television, the internet and live appearances.[43] By associating their identity with a product, the star links their personal brand with another in a mutual self-promotional exchange through which both expect to gain increased visibility and financial rewards. While some celebrities participate regularly in selling products, A-list stars are judicious in choosing brands with which to affiliate and many do not take part in advertising at all. The chosen brand generally conforms to the values represented by the star persona; Kidman's engagement with marketing campaigns is confined to luxury and quality labels such as Omega, Nintendo, Schweppes and Chanel, for whom she has appeared in commercials and related promotional work.[44] Like the activities of the modern commodity star, commercials cross over between different media and entail creative input from people in fashion, film and music. Kidman's Bollywood-style Schweppes commercial, which featured Indian star Arjun Rampal and child actress Rubina Ali, who appeared in *Slumdog Millionaire* (2008), was produced by Ridley Scott and directed by Shekhar Kapur (*Elizabeth*, 1998), while the soundtrack for her Omega Ladymatic commercial was singer-songwriter Simone White's rendition of 'Bunny in a Bunny Suit'.

Her most high-profile appearance is Baz Luhrmann's *No. 5 The Film* (2004), for which she was reputed to have earned the highest fee ever paid to an actress for a commercial.[45] Commercials can be regarded as short films.[46] Perfume commercials, which have become a genre in their own right, are often directed by auteurs and feature major stars.[47] They are devised and produced in the same way as feature-length movies, bear the unmistakable imprint of the director and are listed in their canon of works. Because they are edited for showing in different media, a full-length master copy, or director's cut, often exists; for example, *No. 5 The Film*, envisaged by Luhrmann as a trailer for a film that might have been, was made in a definitive three-minute version for theatrical release that was cut for screening on television. The full version includes one minute of end-credits.[48] Like all Luhrmann's work, the mini-film was treated as a special event designed to attract maximum media coverage. As the face of the Chanel No. 5 label, Kidman took part in an extensive campaign spanning print and audiovisual media that drew on the visual design and imagery of the short film, which was in the mode of Luhrmann's celebrated Red Curtain Trilogy. *No. 5 The Film* brought together several iconic brands: Chanel No. 5, the world's top-selling perfume, associated with glamorous female personalities such as Catherine Deneuve, Jacqueline Kennedy Onassis and Marilyn Monroe; Karl Lagerfeld, controversial head designer for Chanel, who designed Kidman's couture gowns for the commercial; Baz Luhrmann and Catherine Martin, who together were responsible for the style of the Red Curtain films; and Kidman, one of the world's most powerful and bankable stars. This was a potent creative and commercial alliance that promised to consolidate the positions of all concerned. The script echoed the story and romantic themes of *Moulin Rouge!* (2001) and, as with Kidman's performance as Satine, her image consisted of a pastiche of famous women, this time linked with the fragrance.

The action is set in an imaginary locale, a hybrid of Paris and New York, created through special visual effects. Kidman plays 'the most famous woman in the world', who disappears from the glare of the cameras to have a brief affair with a penniless bohemian writer (Rodrigo Santoro) before returning to her former life. In the time spent in the writer's garret, she discards her expensive gown for her lover's shirt, shorts and black jacket, switching from ultra-feminine glamour to dishevelled tomboy. For the final 'red carpet' moment, she wears an elegant, backless, fitted black dress, her blonde hair scraped back into a smooth bun, apparently once again in control of her star image. The diamond necklace that emblazons 'No. 5' on her back is the only emblem of the product that appears in the film, whose relationship to a commercial is equivocal. The role of the perfume in Kidman's journey is obscure, while the ubiquitous Chanel signage that confines her in the city streets is also there on the rooftop garret, with the result that her escape is presented as illusory. *No. 5 The Film* might be seen as an ironic reflection on the

branding process and on Kidman's commodity stardom.[49] The dazzling necklace displays the No. 5 insignia inside a circle so that it resembles the marque used to brand cattle. It hangs from her neck rather like a rein, suggesting restraint. It is as though Kidman is an object stamped by the image-saturated commercial environment she inhabits and entirely defined by it. Her implausible performance underlines her entrapment in an unreal world of surfaces. Luhrmann's mini-film uses Kidman's star persona to question the superficial glamour of the very brands it sets out to promote.

Philanthropy

Philanthropic activities and charitable donations play a significant part in the construction of star personas. Indeed, humanitarian causes and awards feature prominently in the operations of the entertainment industries. A website dedicated to 'the world of celebrity giving' lists 1,702 charities and 2,600 celebrities, posting news of George Clooney's human-rights Satellite Sentinel Project and Ben Affleck's support for the anti-poverty initiative Robin Hood as well as 'charity biographies' for celebrities. Nicole Kidman's entry records her work for UNICEF and UNIFEM, her charity donations and fundraising activities. A roll call of sixteen charities and foundations she has supported includes Artists for Peace and Justice, Global Green Plan and Breast Cancer Care. She is quoted as saying: 'I find trying to solve problems and save lives is far more important than my film career.'[50] Kidman's sponsorship and humanitarian work is Australian and international: from 1993–2002 she was ambassador for the Australian Theatre for Young People (atyp), becoming its patron in 2002. In the 1990s, she was appointed a national Goodwill Ambassador for UNICEF in Australia and in 2006, she became a Goodwill Ambassador for UNIFEM, which supports women's rights and gender equality around the world. In 2009, she lent her voice to the 'Say NO – UNiTE' initiative to end violence against women, speaking in front of the US House Subcommittee on Human Rights.[51] As part of her advocacy for women's rights she travelled to the Democratic Republic of the Congo and Kosovo to talk to victims of violence. In 2006, Kidman was awarded Australia's highest civilian honour Companion of the Order of Australia for her services to the performing arts, youth sponsorship, health-care issues and humanitarian causes.[52] In 2010, she spoke at a ceremony to mark the partnership between the Family Violence Prevention Fund and Say NO.[53] The same year, she and Keith Urban announced plans to fund a school in Haiti and Kidman made a goodwill visit there to meet earthquake survivors and women's rights activists. Together with other celebrities, she participated in a fund-raising telethon to help victims rendered homeless by the Nashville floods, helping to raise $1.7 million.[54]

All these activities involve live and other kinds of performances by Kidman for which she and the various causes (many of which are themselves brands) receive substantial media coverage. Ostensibly she plays herself, portraying a character who prioritises humanitarian issues over career or money. There is a redemptive aspect to stars' philanthropy whereby the rich and famous can be seen to use their power and influence to help those less fortunate. George Clooney is an example of a commodity star whose authenticity resides in his espousal of liberal causes on and off screen. In Kidman's case, human-rights advocacy contributes to building a 'good' character, who is aware of her own luck and wants to give something back. It also strengthens her Australian identity; she frequently traces her commitment to fighting injustice to her parents' social conscience and her work in cancer research to her mother's breast cancer, both of which turn up regularly in her biographical details. In the context of her commodity stardom, it is difficult not to regard Kidman's philanthropic activity as a bid for publicity and as a product for exchange in the market. Despite the fact that she may not profit directly in financial terms, she gains what might be termed 'altruistic capital' that benefits her persona by bolstering her authenticity. Her stardom depends on her status as a special individual; benevolent enterprises bring her out of her exclusive, élite world, forge a connection with a wider society of deserving human beings and attempt to build an affective relationship with consumers.

Her performance in these areas contributes to the sense that there is a unified, knowable person behind the vagaries of her star image and her film roles. Even though her compassion may be motivated partly by career interests, there is no reason to assume that it does not represent genuine concern, or that it does not contribute to social and cultural change. In response to Kidman's role as advocate for Say NO, Janet Street-Porter wrote a scathing piece in the *Independent* heaping scorn on the idea of stars as goodwill

ambassadors and claiming that Kidman's participation in a
misogynist entertainment industry was a betrayal of real women.[55]
This was followed by a more sympathetic article in the *Guardian* by
Samantha Morton praising Kidman's stand against Hollywood's
demeaning portrayal of women and her bravery in speaking out
against studio interests.[56] Both columns had recourse to reality:
Street-Porter inveighed against the degrading fictions perpetrated
by Hollywood and their part in encouraging actual sexual violence
against women, while Morton argued that actresses are real women
who can make responsible choices about the roles they play. The
controversy highlights the conundrums surrounding commodity
stars; the fragmented nature of Kidman's image could encourage the
perception that her philanthropic identity is yet another character in
her portfolio rather than an authentic expression of her real self.
The suspicion that she may be having it both ways is one of the
consequences of her success in creating a multifaceted persona. As
with the conjunction of commerce and art in her career, an unease
exists around the commodification of human kindness as part of the
promotion of her brand.

Persona and identity

The case studies outlined above demonstrate the expansion of
star discourse across many different sites, some of which are
interconnected media networks while others are less official. The
star persona, previously seen as a contradictory entity that circulates
in subsidiary media, has taken on a life of its own and is no longer
secondary to the cinematic performance. Now more protean, it has
dispersed into areas that do not so much offer an invitation to the
cinematic performance, rather, they provide opportunities for direct
access to star images themselves and exploration of consumer
fantasies and emotions. The experience of 'cinema' has become one

of immersion in and interaction with a plethora of commercial and cultural activities, not all of which satisfy corporate interests. Kidman's personal brand is characterised by versatility, while the ways in which it is disseminated and consumed are equally varied. This gives her persona an elusive quality, although because of the sheer proliferation of images and the extent of her commodification she can hardly be perceived as enigmatic. Instead, her pervasive presence in diverse forms foregrounds the construction of a mutable character that can satisfy divergent market needs and consumer desires.

This intangible quality is at the heart of her commodification; however, there is another, equally important aspect to her public persona that strives to represent her as more ordinary and human. A familiar backstory is reiterated and, by a process of repetition, gains credibility as truth. The backstory covers significant life events and it returns frequently to Kidman's Australian childhood, which is seen as the key to her personality. In interviews the same anecdotes from her past recur in an attempt to establish a foundation for the shifting persona. Through this process, the star appears to have a coherent individual identity even though very little hard information is offered to the consumer. This identity, while it appears to personify the real Kidman, is both a fiction and a commodity. Like other manifestations of her image, it has symbolic and narrative dimensions as well as promotional functions. In this section, I explore the way Kidman's Australian backstory is used to produce a credible character. The construction of a global brand for a star ensures that they can sell themselves and products in world markets. Many scholars have noted the significance of local and niche contexts in global marketing initiatives.[57] In the construction of Kidman's stardom, her Australian heritage and the values presumed to emanate from it inflect her glamorous Hollywood image producing a narrative that traces a journey from local personality to global mega-star.

National identity

The discourse of national identity is one of the means used to ground Kidman's star persona. Her Australian background is a privileged part of her biography and in the past Sydney has been said to be where her heart is.[58] More recently she declared her intention not to live there because of attention from the paparazzi.[59] Australia can no longer provide a 'home' for the star even though she has family and friends there. As a globe-trotting celebrity she has property in more than one continent and, since her marriage to country-music singer Keith Urban, a New Zealand-born Australian, has emphasised the importance of their Nashville ranch as a place in which to settle. The ranch represents a refuge from the exigencies of fame; it is sometimes characterised as a farm, a place where she can enjoy nature and find peace. As discussed, Kidman's recent pastoral turn was part of re-branding her image and involved conjuring up elements of her youthful identity. It is the Nashville home rather than the Australia of Kidman's childhood and young adult years that constitutes a nostalgic utopian space outside the hurly-burly of the global entertainment industries to which both Kidman and Urban belong. As a private haven, it is an imaginary creation that plays an important role in the projection of Kidman's character as a hard-working professional woman seeking fulfilment outside work. It would appear, then, to be a global metaphor that transcends its local context. As a kind of settlement where she grows organic vegetables and raises animals, it echoes the dreams and aspirations of the homesteaders who colonised Australia and the US (in addition to strengthening her green credentials).[60] Hovering around the vision of an Arcadian paradise is the spectre of national history and identity whose manifestation is dual, reflecting Kidman's US–Australian citizenship.[61]

Kidman's dual citizenship is important to the construction of a mobile global persona. However, her local Australian background, of which she professes to be very proud, provides the basis for distinctive character traits. She is variously described as wilful, independent, flirtatious, loyal, honest, industrious, reckless, down-to-earth, enterprising, adventurous, opinionated and ambitious; many of these characteristics are affiliated with, although not confined to, the forging of Australian colonial nationhood. Her tomboy athleticism is identified with Australian sporting prowess, while a certain naivety in her outlook is associated with Australia's status as a young nation.[62] These traits are both general and specific, defining her as culturally other while allowing for identification with her persona. Despite her pride in her origins, Kidman's Australian backstory depicts her as not entirely comfortable there. Her unusual appearance (height, fair skin and mass of red hair) is said to have singled her out as a child and led to her feeling isolated. This sense of her as different within her home culture creates a type that is both special and ordinary, set apart from and yet connected to others through emotional vulnerability. It also serves to explain her drive as an actress to immerse herself in other identities in her search for one of her own. The story of her Australian roots draws on national stereotypes to endow her character's life journey with a patina of psychological depth. It positions her as non-Hollywood, as a heroic outsider who has succeeded in confounding cultural expectations.

Femininity and beauty

In her study of Australia's configuration of the 1920s modern woman, Liz Conor views this phenomenon as an effect of new visual technologies that produced the New Woman as spectacular public image organised around a series of types: the City or Business Girl; Screen Star; Beauty Contestant; and Flapper.[63] Drawing on Judith Butler's theories of gender performance, Conor sees femininity as the result of repetitive enactment of socially prescribed identities. This emphasis on masquerade envisages the feminine as exhibited through visual display rather than emanating from a predefined self. Conor argues that the invitation to modern women to articulate themselves as spectacles was a transnational global movement, in which Australia participated in its attempt to define a postcolonial identity characterised as white.[64] Conor's analysis is historically grounded; nevertheless, her understanding of 1920s commodified visual culture resonates with Kidman's position within the contemporary entertainment industries and their increased focus on performance, public visibility, consumerism and spectacle. In particular, the ideas of mutable identities and self-representation associated by Conor with modern femininity chime with Kidman's occupation of multiple images in her performance of celebrity stardom. The diverse meanings attached to femininity in Conor's account, such as artificiality, heterosexual appeal, celebrity, commodity display, fashion, youth and scandal are replicated in Kidman's performance of herself.[65]

Conor's description locates feminine agency in self-presentation and engagement with visual culture. This entails the achievement of 'beauty prowess', the mastery of techniques to appear attractive offered by the beauty industries.[66] Kidman's beauty prowess is one of the fundamental elements of her persona; it underlies her public image from the beginning, when her star quality was defined as residing in her photogenic allure. Her modern identity is created, performed and transformed through learned processes of interaction with images, roles and technologies. It is this spectacular self, traversing multiple guises, that manifests her power and invites consumers to identify with her accomplishment of visual perfection. At the same time, the manipulation of types, images and techniques of representation associated with the construction of modern femininity has postcolonial implications in its unsettling of essential identities and emphasis on malleable selves. While Kidman's construction of beauty remains within the boundaries of commodification, it occasionally tests those limits by displaying what could be described as Australian attitude, complying with notions of her as an adventurous and risk-taking character. Her tomboy side allows her to challenge perceptions of ideal feminine beauty by parading androgynous or subcultural styles that intimate representations of glamour appealing to more marginal tastes. By drawing attention to the performative nature of gender, like the Flapper described by Conor, she playfully denaturalises femininity.[67]

Whiteness

Conor's analysis of Australian 1920s womanhood reveals that it was constructed as specifically white European and modelled on classical standards of beauty.[68] She argues that this colonial conception effaced the nation's pre-settlement history, denying the land theft on which it was founded and excluding Aboriginal women from modernity.[69] By deconstructing the racialised discourses that produced Australian femininity as a founding principle of nationhood, Conor's work participates in the project of whiteness studies to critique whiteness as a cultural norm and understand its local manifestations.[70] In such work, the privilege and power attached to whiteness are defamiliarised and its authority displaced. In his investigation of whiteness as a racial category, Richard Dyer identifies some of the meanings attached to it, including spirituality, purity, superiority, energy, enterprise, progress, modernity and discipline, and their mobilisation in colonial ventures.[71] For Dyer, white imperialism validates itself in specific ways through notions of the body as taut and lean, disciplined through diet and training and kept in check. Through this disciplined body, whiteness is perceived to transcend the corporeal and attains spiritual status.[72] Dyer identifies the ambiguity surrounding white women in colonial discourse, who are both bearers of privilege and excluded from exercising power.[73] He sees the active attributes assigned to white imperialist enterprise as confined to men. In representing true whiteness, white women inspire male narrative action rather than engage in it themselves.

These studies open up whiteness to critical enquiry, laying bare many of the implicit assumptions that shore up its representational potency. They help to shed light on the nature of Kidman's whiteness, which is one of the marked elements of her persona. Her beauty is overtly coded as white and, as noted, some aspects of her character are affiliated with white European colonial activity in Australia. Dyer's description of the disciplined bodies associated with imperialism resonates with Kidman's lean, trained, white physique while the connotations of whiteness, such as energy, progress, modernity and enterprise, are part of her identity. If Dyer is right to argue that white women inspire male action rather than act independently themselves, then Kidman's white persona would seem to transgress one of the tenets of white colonialism by taking on the attributes of white colonial masculinity. Conor's local research nuances Dyer's argument by demonstrating that in the beauty culture of 1920s Australia, some of those attributes migrated to conceptions of modern Australian femininity, which was allied to the national image of the male 'digger'.[74] Kidman's persona emerges from this context of Australian postcolonial culture, in which white European women were positioned as active participants in nation-building. As Conor indicates, such nationalist projections effaced colonial history and marginalised indigenous women. But, if Kidman's whiteness could be seen as contaminated by imperialism, its meaning is not fixed.

Conor and Dyer point out that ideas of whiteness are produced through performance and technologies of make-up, lighting and photography and are specific to context. Kidman's white skin appears in diverse forms and arenas. On the cover of the October 2007 issue of *Vanity Fair*, she bares her chest to reveal a white bra underneath a white shirt, wearing a white sailor cap atop her long blonde hair. In this case there is an irony in the conjunction of titillating exposure of flawless skin, of which little is actually shown, and the virtue implied by the pristine whiteness of her outfit. Inside, an advert for Omega watches displays a head-and-shoulders shot of Kidman wearing a skimpy white slip in which her unblemished pale skin appears almost translucent and her blue eyes and blonde curls are emphasised. She seems to radiate light like the bejewelled gold watch in the foreground so that both are conveyed as objects of matchless beauty. Here, her whiteness has an ethereal, transcendental quality that equates the watch with Kidman's visual perfection.[75] The image's Aryan connotations are offset by the fact that it exudes a visual excess that is clearly mechanically produced and so reveals its status as pure image. In her idealised whiteness, Kidman comes across as a manufactured artefact in what might be read as an oblique reflection on her value as a commodity. For her role as Satine in *Moulin Rouge!*, Kidman's skin is lit with blue light to appear deathly white, anticipating her character's demise but also intimating her own iconicity. In *The Others* (*Los otros*, 2001), her white skin is used to create a sense of her character's strangeness and alienation, while in *Australia* (2008) it connotes Lady Sarah Ashley's class, race and cultural difference. In these cases, Kidman could be said to perform whiteness.[76] Although such ambiguous strategies may not achieve the 'making whiteness strange' called for by Dyer,[77] they indicate that, as a feature of her star identity and as a commodity, Kidman's white beauty is not normalised.

Indeed, it is presented as extraordinary. In interviews her paleness is remarked on with such regularity that it has become a trademark and the words 'porcelain skin' are frequently used in descriptions of her.[78] It is also a topic for discussion: for example, in the extreme heat she experienced while filming *Australia*, her fair complexion was a disadvantage. Despite the fact that over the last thirty or so years the much-discussed whiteness of mainstream

Deathly white: Nicole Kidman as Satine in
Moulin Rouge!

Hollywood has come under pressure from an influx of black actors and film-makers, white stars and white-centred narratives predominate and whiteness remains a paramount indicator of value. In this context, Kidman's deployment of whiteness as a distinguishing feature of her persona participates in commodity exchange. At the same time, its very prominence renders it, if not strange, at least visible. Its variable use in different circumstances of production and consumption facilitates a proliferation of meanings; while some exploit less progressive aspects of Kidman's whiteness, others may work to problematise or undermine its connotations of power and privilege.

Feminism

Like other aspects of her persona, Kidman's feminism is controversial and contested. As a commodity star, she uses her beauty and sexuality for commercial purposes. From *Dead Calm* (1989) to *The Hours, Dogville* (2003) and *Birth*, she is identified with conflicted heroines whose feminist motivations are far from clear, while her performances in postfeminist re-makes such as *The Stepford Wives* (2004) and *Bewitched* (2005) have been associated with a backlash.[79] In contrast to these ambiguous renditions, Kidman unequivocally asserts her feminist politics in her work as UNIFEM advocate, paying tribute to her mother Janelle, a second-wave feminist, as an inspiration. Although a dichotomy between the actress's dramatic roles and the 'real' Kidman might be mobilised to explain these apparent inconsistencies, such a perception does not hold up when her identity is considered as a fiction. In this light, it makes more sense to understand Kidman's performance of feminism as an engagement with the women's movement defined in terms of conflicting ideologies rather than as unified. The notions of feminism as performance and of the women's movement as lacking a central

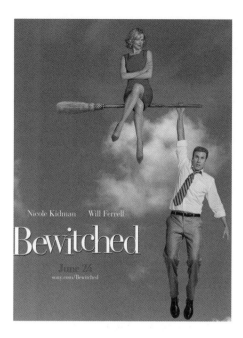

Postfeminist update:
Nicole Kidman and Will Ferrell
in *Bewitched*

organising principle risk sacrificing authenticity, history and political credibility. Nevertheless, in the context of contemporary media cultures, where the search for authenticity is both intensified and confounded, they are helpful in illuminating the ways in which feminism has mutated in response to cultural change. Kidman's performance of feminism does not derive from direct involvement with women's-movement politics; rather, as part of her public persona, she is an advocate for feminism.

At the beginning of an article by Sherryl Vint appraising *The Stepford Wives* and *Bewitched* as examples of a new feminist backlash, a large head-and-shoulders glamour photograph of Kidman appears in which she is looking into camera with a vacuous smile. The image is used to epitomise her postfeminist roles and the article includes two other photographs of her in which her glitzy, ultra-feminine appearance is displayed. Vint focuses on narrative exposition and, in the absence of detailed analysis of Kidman's performance in either film, the images imply her complicity with the postfeminist agenda of undermining the politics and achievements of second-wave feminism. For Vint, the new backlash movies ridicule feminism, evacuating political consciousness and positing heterosexual love as a solution to gender inequality. She aligns them with third-wave feminism, which she sees as envisaging female empowerment through personal choice and individual interaction with consumerism and sexual display.[80] In the interests of her polemic, Vint underestimates the contribution of performance in producing a distance on the films' postfeminism, which mitigates their backlash status to some extent. However, her argument is part of a wider discussion about feminism(s) that usefully outlines the landscape of dissension and debate against which Kidman's enactment of feminism is played out.

Kidman's feminism emerges from her Australian background. Her mother's influence connects her to the 1960s and 1970s local women's movement, while the woman-centred narratives and independent heroines of her 1980s career are linked to the Australian industry's support for women film-makers and the existence of a strong national feminist movement.[81] Within her life story, her journey from local success to international stardom positions her as a positive heroine whose accomplishments are honoured at home and abroad. Her power and influence span many different areas of creativity as well as being realised in terms of substantial personal wealth. She has attained fulfilment in domestic and professional realms, and her resilience in the face of private and career troubles adds to her heroism. Although stardom removes her from the world of ordinary mortals, her Australian identity, as the basis of her persona, provides her with typical characteristics and values. She is seen as a national ambassador and celebrated for her international triumphs. To many she represents a pinnacle of female achievement, a living example of the values of hard work, enterprise and professionalism, who combines beauty and intelligence with talent. She has guaranteed her cultural impact as much through her ability to negotiate the complex operations of the global entertainment industries and the demands of commodity stardom as through acclaim for her film and theatre acting.

Kidman's feminist identity is complicated by her need as an actress and celebrity to remain attuned to market demands. Over the years, her persona has responded to changes in consumer tastes in order to survive. She attaches herself to film and commercial projects that do not necessarily enhance her feminist credibility but may ensure the visibility she needs in the industry and the eyes of the public. This can be seen as complicity with market forces; but it is also a sign of strategic intelligence. Her reputation for shrewdness and instinct for power are advantages in a high-risk business environment and, while many would see her willingness to negotiate the processes of commodification as antipathetic to feminism, her life and career dramatise the advantages and perils experienced by women who navigate the precarious terrain of contemporary celebrity stardom. Some of these activities may be troublesome for traditional feminisms, but they throw into relief the contested, dynamic and evolving nature of feminism itself.

* * *

My analysis of Nicole Kidman's commodity stardom reveals the extent and limitations of star agency and control in the context of the modern global media industries. While the freelance package system offers stars greater power and influence, not to mention financial rewards, they are required to respond to the vagaries of market-led policies and the unpredictable nature of consumer tastes in order to survive. This results in strategic decisions that, whatever their intentions, do not necessarily enhance their reputation artistically or in the eyes of the public. As idealised figures, stars are the focus for

Success as producer and star: Nicole Kidman
in *Rabbit Hole*

myriad fantasies and desires, including political aspirations. Their
imbrication in commodity exchange does not exclude engagement
with politics, as Kidman's encapsulation of glamour, commerce, art
and feminism demonstrates. However, while this combination is
appreciated by fans, it is regarded with suspicion by those for whom
it does not cohere into an ideal. This uneasy situation feeds into the
culture of discussion and dispute that characterises modern star
discourse, feeding controversy and courting visibility across different
media.

Kidman's career to date is defined by her ability to manage the
conflicting personal and professional demands of commodity
stardom and the commercial imperatives of the entertainment
industry. Her star power shows no signs of waning; she plans to
repeat her success as actress and producer on *Rabbit Hole* (2010)
with projects for Blossom Films such as *The Danish Girl*, in which
she will play a male-to-female transsexual as well as produce. At the

time of writing, this controversial project, which was due to start shooting in summer 2011, has stalled; two directors and a succession of female stars who were to play opposite Kidman have left. Despite her status as a box-office draw, as an independent film-maker, even with the support of major studio Fox, Kidman is vulnerable to the intensely competitive industrial climate. She is also at the mercy of swings in audience response. Her move into production may be motivated by a desire to secure creative control, enabling her to choose projects and directors; as the example of *The Danish Girl* indicates, her agency in this respect is circumscribed. In acting terms, her future roles are increasingly determined by her age: it was announced in 2011 that she would appear with James Franco in a Broadway revival of Tennessee Williams's *Sweet Bird of Youth*.[82] It is impossible to predict whether such strategies will serve to consolidate her position, but they manifest the keen business sense, adventurous spirit and determination to survive characteristic of the Nicole Kidman persona.

NOTES

Introduction

1 Richard Dyer, *Stars* (London: BFI, 1998), p. 34; Paul McDonald, *The Star System: Hollywood's Production of Popular Identities* (London: Wallflower Press, 2000), pp. 5–14; Christine Geraghty, 'Re-examining Stardom: Questions of Texts, Bodies and Performance', in Christine Gledhill and Linda Williams (eds), *Reinventing Film Studies* (London: Arnold, 2000), p. 184.

2 See Christine Geraghty, 'Crossing Over: Performing as a Lady and a Dame', *Screen* vol. 43 no. 1, Spring 2002, pp. 41–2.

1 Stardom

1 For example, John Ellis, 'Stars as a Cinematic Phenomenon', in *Visible Fictions: Cinema, Television, Video* (London and New York: Routledge, 1992), p. 91.

2 Richard Dyer, *Heavenly Bodies: Film Stars and Society* (London and New York: Routledge, 2004), p. 3.

3 Dyer, *Heavenly Bodies*, p. 10.

4 Dyer, *Heavenly Bodies*, pp. 10 ff.

5 Liz Conor, 'Nicole Kidman and the Commodity Star', *Metro* vol. 127 no. 8, April 2001, pp. 98–9.

6   See Joshua Gamson, *Claims to Fame: Celebrity in Modern America* (Berkeley: University of California Press, 1994).

7   See also Richard DeCordova, *Picture Personalities: The Emergence of the Star System in America* (Champaign: University of Illinois Press, 2001), pp. 85–8.

8   Jeannette Delamoir, 'Eyes Wide Shut: Tom, Nicole, Stardom and Visual Memory', *Transformations* no. 3, June 2002. Available online: <http://www.transformationsjournal.org/journal/issue_03/editorial.shtml>. Accessed 10 February 2011.

9   Delamoir, 'Eyes Wide Shut', p. 1.

10 Nicole Kidman married country singer Keith Urban in June 2006. Tom Cruise married actress Katie Holmes in November 2006. Both weddings were high-profile celebrity events.

11 Ellis discusses the present-yet-absent quality of stars and its relationship to the film performance in *Visible Fictions*, pp. 99 ff.

12 Email dated 3 February 2011 from atyp archivist Judith Seeff. Nicole Kidman was atyp ambassador from 1993–2002 and atyp patron from 2002–9.

13 Kidman played Annie in Season Three, which aired on the Disney Channel between January and August 1985. According to the IMDb she appeared in twelve episodes: <http://www.imdb.com/title/tt0086714>. Accessed 18 February 2011.

14 'Bop Girl' music video can be viewed on YouTube: <http://www.youtube.com/watch?v=Mg1HTNrDA1Y>. Accessed 18 February 2011.

15 See Debbie Kruger, 'The Art of Growing Up as an Actress', *Australian*, 1 December 1986. Available online: <http://www.debbiekruger.com/writer/freelance/nic.html>. Accessed 18 February 2011.

16 Daphne Guinness, 'Candid Camera', *Sydney Morning Herald*, 15 September 2004. Available online: <http://www.smh.com.au/articles/2004/09/14/1094927575718.html?from=storylhs>. Accessed 18 February 2011.

17 Kruger, 'The Art of Growing Up as an Actress'.

18 Kruger, 'The Art of Growing Up as an Actress'.

19 See screen-capture images on *Five Mile Creek* unofficial website:
    <http://www.fivemilecreek.net/show/photo/screencaps/annie.htm>.
    Accessed 22 February 2011.

20 See clip from *Archer* on YouTube: <http://www.youtube.com/
    watch?v=dm8v-zGQYiA&feature=related>. Accessed 22 February
    2011.

21 Kidman received the 1988 AFI award for Best Actress in a Leading Role
    in a Television Drama: <http://www.imdb.com/name/nm0000173/
    awards>. Accessed 22 February 2011.

22 I discuss performance in depth in Chapter 2.

23 See IMDb: <http://www.imdb.com/title/tt0097162/companycredits>.

24 For example, Jonathan Rayner, *Contemporary Australian Cinema: An
    Introduction* (Manchester: Manchester University Press, 2000), p. 169,
    sees *Dead Calm* as a step back from Noyce's works of social criticism
    Newsfront (1979) and *Heatwave* (1982).

25 See Tom O'Regan, *Australian National Cinema* (London and New York:
    Routledge, 1996), p. 56.

26 See John O'Donnell, 'Flaming Star', *Rolling Stone* (Australia) no. 432,
    June 1989, pp. 38–42, 98.

27 David Thomson, *Nicole Kidman* (London: Bloomsbury, 2006), p. 34.
    Caveat: Thomson's biography has neither notes nor references, so most
    of his information is unsubstantiated.

28 See Paul McDonald, *The Star System: Hollywood's Production of Popular
    Identities* (London: Wallflower Press, 2000), p. 97.

29 IMDb gives the budget for *Days of Thunder* as $60 million – a figure far
    in excess of Cruise's projects so far: <http://www.imdb.com/title/
    tt0099371/business>. Accessed 24 February 2011.

30 Thomson, *Nicole Kidman*, p. 49, claims Kidman's fee was $200,000
    while Cruise earned $10 million.

31 IMDb gives gross US earnings as $82,670,733: <http://www.imdb.com/
    title/tt0099371/business>. Accessed 24 February 2011.

32 See Roger Ebert, *Chicago Sun-Times*; Peter Travers, *Rolling Stone*; Hal
    Hinson, *Washington Post*; and Desson Howe, *Washington Post* at IMDb:

<http://www.imdb.com/title/tt0099371/externalreviews>. Accessed
24 February 2011.

33 See feature article and interview by Christopher Hunt, 'Nicole Kidman:
The Princess Bride', *Movieline*, July 1991, pp. 44–8, 85–6. Available
online: <http://www.movieline.com/1991/07/nicole-kidman-the-
princess-bride.php?page=all>. Accessed 24 February 2011.

34 See interview by Stephen Rebello, '60 Minutes with Tom Cruise',
Movieline, December 1992, pp. 30–5, 78, 80, 84. Available online:
<http://www.movieline.com/1992/12/60-minutes-with-tom-cruise.php>.
Accessed 25 February 2011.

35 Stephen Rebello, 'Nicole Kidman: Nic of Time', *Movieline*, March 1994,
pp. 30–4, 81–3, 85. Available online: <http://www.movieline.com/1994/
03/nic-of-time.php>. Accessed 25 February 2011.

36 Rebello, 'Nicole Kidman', p. 83.

37 Dyer, *Heavenly Bodies*, p. 143. Delamoir, 'Eyes Wide Shut', p. 7.

38 Rebello, 'Nicole Kidman', p. 82.

39 See Pam Cook, *Baz Luhrmann* (London: BFI, 2010), p. 25.

40 *Vogue* (Australia), January 1994. The issue also featured Kylie Minogue
as 'Judy L'Amour', who appeared on the cover. Clips from this issue of
Vogue appear in the Red Curtain segment on the Behind the Red Curtain
bonus disc in *Baz Luhrmann's Red Curtain Trilogy* boxed set.

41 McDonald, *The Star System*, pp. 93–6.

42 See Conor, 'Nicole Kidman and the Commodity Star', p. 99.

43 See Dennis Bingham, 'Kidman, Cruise and Kubrick: A Brechtian
Pastiche', in Cynthia Baron, Diane Carson and Frank P. Tomasulo (eds),
*More Than a Method: Trends and Traditions in Contemporary Film
Performance* (Detroit, MI: Wayne State University Press, 2004).

44 See pp. 68–9.

45 See Leslie Bennetts, 'La Femme Nicole', *Vanity Fair*, July 1995, pp. 62–9,
128; Jamie Diamond, 'Nicole Springs Forward', *Vogue*, February 1995,
pp. 202–13.

46 For example, Janet Maslin, 'She Trusts in TV's Redeeming Power',
New York Times, 27 September 1995. Available online: <http://movies.

nytimes.com/movie/review?res=990CEFDC103BF934A1575AC0A963
958260>. Accessed 7 March 2011; Mick LaSalle, 'Kidman Monstrously
Good in "To Die For"', *San Francisco Chronicle*, 6 October 1995, p. C-3.
Available online: <http://www.sfgate.com/cgi-bin/article.cgi?f=/c/a/
1995/10/06/DD13291.DTL>. Accessed 7 March 2011.

47 Bob Strauss, 'A Role to Die For', *Los Angeles Daily News*, 5 October
1995. Available online: <http://articles.sun-sentinel.com/1995-10-
05/lifestyle/9510040328_1_suzanne-stone-nicole-kidman-drugstore-
cowboy>. Accessed 7 March 2011.

48 IMDb has full awards history for *To Die For*: <http://www.imdb.com/title/
tt0114681/awards>. Accessed 7 March 2011.

49 For example, Bennetts, 'La Femme Nicole', p. 68. The couple adopted
Isabella Jane in 1992 and Connor Antony in 1995.

50 Jane Campion's *The Piano* (1993) was a commercial and critical success.

51 See Roger Ebert, '*The Portrait of a Lady*', *Chicago Sun-Times*, 17 January
1997. Available online: <http://rogerebert.suntimes.com/apps/pbcs.dll/
article?AID=/19970117/REVIEWS/701170304/1023>. Accessed
8 March 2011. Edward Guthmann, 'Arty "Portrait" Loaded with Heavy
Symbolism', *San Francisco Chronicle*, 17 January 1997, p. D-3. Available
online: <http://www.sfgate.com/cgi-bin/article.cgi?f=/c/a/1997/01/17/
DD63103.DTL>. Accessed 8 March 2011.

52 Michael Shnayerson, 'Portrait of an Actress: Nicole Kidman's
Remarkable Year', *Vanity Fair* no. 446, October 1997, pp. 198, 225–7.

53 According to Thomson, *Nicole Kidman*, p. 125.

54 Kidman was nominated for the Best Actress Laurence Olivier Award and
won the *Evening Standard* Award for Unique Contribution to London
Theatre. See <http://www.iainglen.com/the-blue-room.php>, which
includes contemporary reviews. Accessed 9 March 2011.

55 See Ben Brantley, 'Fool's Gold in the Kingdom of Desire', *New York
Times*, 14 December 1998. Available online: <http://theater.nytimes.com/
mem/theater/treview.html?html_title=&tols_title=blue%20room,%20the
%20(play)&pdate=19981214&byline=by%20ben%20brantley&id=1077
011432284>. Accessed 9 March 2011.

56 John Powers, 'Portraits of a Lady', *Vogue*, June 1999, p. 214.

57 For example, Gamson, *Claims to Fame*, pp. 57–78.

58 See P. David Marshall, *Celebrity and Power: Fame in Contemporary Culture* (Minneapolis: University of Minnesota Press, 1997), p. 68. Also Delamoir, 'Eyes Wide Shut'.

59 McDonald, *The Star System*, pp. 113–15, discusses the impact of the internet on stardom. One example is the fan website, which produces an unofficial archive of materials that construct a particular story, and an identity for the star. Another example is the practice of posting clips and star tributes on YouTube, in which mini-narratives are created.

60 See Sharon Waxman, 'How Personal Is Too Personal for a Star Like Tom Cruise?', *New York Times*, 2 June 2005. Available online: <http://www.nytimes.com/2005/06/02/movies/02crui.html?_r=1&ex=1275364800&en=5bee0745ec59eea3&ei=5090&partner=rssuserland&emc=rss>. Accessed 10 March 2011.

61 See BBC News report: 'Cruise and Kidman Win Libel Case', 29 October 1998. Available online: <http://news.bbc.co.uk/1/hi/entertainment/203779.stm>. Accessed 10 March 2011.

62 Powers, 'Portraits of a Lady', p. 215.

63 In 1993, Cruise set up an independent company Cruise/Wagner Productions, which had an exclusive deal with Paramount until 2006. Cruise/Wagner's first production was *Mission: Impossible* (1996), which was Cruise's first production credit.

64 Some sources report that Cruise sued the London tabloid the *Star* for asserting that he and Kidman required a sex counsellor to help them with love-making scenes in *Eyes Wide Shut*. See 'Tom Cruise Timeline' at: <http://www.twoop.com/people/tom_cruise.html>. Accessed 10 March 2011. Also Powers, 'Portraits of a Lady', p. 215.

65 McDonald, *The Star System*, p. 112.

66 As Thomson, *Nicole Kidman*, p. 105, suggests.

67 *Eyes Wide Shut* is discussed in depth in Chapter 2. See pp. 52–9.

68 See Powers, 'Portraits of a Lady', p. 215. The couple separated at the end of 2000. Their divorce was finalised in 2001.

69 Delamoir, '*Eyes Wide Shut*', pp. 2–4.

70 Delamoir, '*Eyes Wide Shut*', pp. 6–8.

71 See Cook, *Baz Luhrmann*, p. 102.

72 See Ingrid Sischy, 'Nicole's New Light', *Vanity Fair* no. 508, December 2002, pp. 204–11, 244–7.

73 See Sischy, 'Nicole's New Light', compared with Powers, 'Portraits of a Lady', in which she was photographed in the style of portrait painter John Singer Sargent.

74 Justin Wyatt, 'The Formation of the "Major Independent": Miramax, New Line and the New Hollywood', in Steve Neale and Murray Smith (eds), *Contemporary Hollywood Cinema* (London and New York: Routledge, 1998).

75 See Cook, *Baz Luhrmann*, p. 26, for discussion of 'creative capital'.

76 According to IMDb, Kidman sings 'I Only Have Eyes for You' (uncredited) in *The Others*, and 'Somethin' Stupid' with Robbie Williams in *Birthday Girl*. The latter was released as a music video in 2001.

77 *The Hours* is discussed in Chapter 2.

78 See Michael Cunningham, 'Nicole Kidman', *Interview*, February 2002, pp. 92–101; Charlotte Chandler, 'Nicole', *Another Magazine* no. 4, Spring/Summer 2003, pp. 148–60.

79 See Daisy Garnett, 'Dramatic Leanings', *Harper's Bazaar*, 1 September 2001. The cover carries a sultry photo of Kidman with the byline: 'Nicole Kidman reveals her closet secrets'.

80 See, for example, Nino Oxilia's *Rapsodia Satanica* (1917), for which Italian fashion designer Mariano Fortuny provided the costumes for diva Lyda Borelli. Fashion's relationship to stardom is discussed further in Chapter 3.

81 See Julie Neigher, 'Oscar Fashion's Back Story', *Los Angeles Times* Image section, 28 February 2010.

82 See Chapter 3, pp. 87–90.

83 An argument made by Thomson, *Nicole Kidman*, pp. 208, 211.

84 *No. 5 The Film* is analysed by Cook, *Baz Luhrmann*, pp. 110–15.

85 For example, Peter Travers, *Rolling Stone* no. 960, 28 October 2004. Available online: <http://www.rollingstone.com/movies/reviews/birth-20041028>. Accessed 16 March 2011.

86 See Reuters report dated 29 November 2006: 'Kidman Is Now the Highest Paid Actress', at *Today.com*: <http://today.msnbc.msn.com/id/15958023>. Accessed 16 March 2011.

87 See Ruthe Stein, 'Arbus Biopic Gets a Little Too Hairy', *San Francisco Chronicle*, 17 November 2006, p. E-4. Available online: <http://www.sfgate.com/cgi-bin/article.cgi?f=/c/a/2006/11/17/DDGQKMDLMS1.DTL>. Accessed 16 March 2011. Also David Thomson, 'Nicole at Forty', *Sunday Times* Culture section, 17 September 2006.

88 See Nicole LaPorte and Gabriel Snyder, 'Shingle Blooms at Fox', *Variety*, 4 April 2006. The first-look deal allows Fox to be the first to accept or decline involvement in any of Blossom Films' projects.

89 See David Thomson, 'Nicole Kidman Is Queen of the Flops', *Guardian*, 8 December 2008. Available online: <http://www.guardian.co.uk/film/filmblog/2008/dec/08/nicole-kidman-angelina-jolie>. Accessed 17 March 2011.

90 See McDonald, *The Star System*, pp. 108–10.

91 See Alex Dobuzinskis, 'Jolie Tops Hollywood Earnings League for Women', *Guardian*, 8 December 2008. Available online: <http://www.guardian.co.uk/film/2008/dec/08/angelina-jolie-tops-earnings-chart>. Accessed 17 March 2011.

92 *Australia* is discussed in Chapter 2. See pp. 64–70.

93 See Rebecca Davies, 'A-listers "Take Recession Pay Cuts"', *Digital Spy*, 10 August 2009. Available online: <http://www.digitalspy.ie/movies/news/a170367/a-listers-take-recession-paycuts.html>. Accessed 17 March 2011.

94 Christopher Goodwin, 'Hollywood Signals Death of the Star System', *First Post*, 3 April 2009. Available online: <http://www.thefirstpost.co.uk/33807,news-comment,news-politics,hollywood-signals-death-of-the-star-system>. Accessed 17 March 2011.

95 'Kidman Still among Hollywood's Top Earners', *WAtoday*, 4 July 2009. Available online: <http://www.watoday.com.au/world/kidman-still-among-hollywoods-top-earners-20090703-d7ri.html>. Accessed 17 March 2011.

96 'Kidman Slips from Ranks of Hollywood's Top Earning Actresses', *Australian*, 4 August 2010. Available online: <http://www.theaustralian.com.au/news/arts/nicole-kidman-slips-from-ranks-of-hollywoods-top-earning-actresses/story-e6frg8n6-1225901261940>. Accessed 17 March 2011.

97 There are two main Nicole Kidman fan websites: *Nicole's Magic* and *Nicole Kidman United*. Nicole Kidman has an official website at: <http://www.nicolekidmanofficial.com/>, accessed 18 March 2011, and a Facebook page.

98 See Stewart Heritage, 'Can Nicole Kidman Pull an Oscar out of a Rabbit Hole?', *Guardian*, 27 October 2010. Available online: <http://www.guardian.co.uk/film/filmblog/2010/oct/27/nicole-kidman-oscar-rabbit-hole>. Accessed 18 March 2011. Also Willa Paskin, 'Nicole Kidman's Forehead Is Back!: An Animated Retrospective', *New York Magazine Vulture Section*, 15 December 2010. Available at: <http://nymag.com/daily/entertainment/2010/12/we_warmly_welcome_back_nicole.html>. Accessed 18 March 2011.

99 See Paul Lieberman, 'Nicole Kidman Finds a New Passion for Her Craft', *Los Angeles Times*, The Envelope section, 7 November 2007, S. 31. Also Krista Smith, 'The Lady Is Yar', *Vanity Fair* no. 566, October 2007, p. 243.

100 For example, John Powers, 'Days of Heaven', *Vogue* [US], July 2008, pp. 116–31.

101 See Nikki Finke, 'Nicole Kidman Hires Angelina's Manager', *Deadline Hollywood*, 22 January 2010. Available online: <http://www.deadline.com/2010/01/nicole-signs-with-angelinas-manager/>. Accessed 18 March 2011.

102 See Aaron Parsley, 'Nicole Kidman: I Used Botox But Didn't Like It', *People*, 12 January 2011. Available online: <http://www.people.com/

people/article/0,,20457031,00.html?xid=rss-topheadlines&utm_source=
feedburner&utm_medium=feed&utm_campaign=Feed%3A+people%2
Fheadlines+%28PEOPLE.com%3A+Top+Headlines%29>. Accessed
18 March 2011.

103 Jennifer Aniston, 'Nicole Kidman: The Interview', *Harper's Bazaar*,
5 January 2011. Available online: <http://www.harpersbazaar.com/
magazine/cover/nicole-kidman-interview-0211>. Accessed 18 March
2011.

104 Mick LaSalle, '*Rabbit Hole* Review: Sad Event, Stultifying Film', *San
Francisco Chronicle*, 24 December 2010. Available online: <http://articles.
sfgate.com/2010-12-24/entertainment/25547416_1_rabbit-hole-movie-
review-david-lindsay-abaire>. Accessed 18 March 2011.

105 See UNIFEM page on Nicole Kidman official website:
<http://www.nicolekidmanofficial.com/about-unifem/>. Accessed
18 March 2011.

106 Willa Paskin and Claude Brodesser-Akner, 'The Star Market: Can *Rabbit
Hole* Help Nicole Kidman Reconnect with Audiences?', *New York
Magazine Vulture Section*, 24 December 2010. Available online:
<http://nymag.com/daily/entertainment/2010/12/nicole_kidman_star_
market.html>. Accessed 18 March 2011.

2 Performance

1 See Philip Drake, 'Reconceptualizing Screen Performance', *Journal of
Film and Video* vol. 58 nos 1–2, Spring/Summer 2006, p. 85.

2 See also Christine Geraghty, 'Crossing Over: Performing as a Lady and a
Dame', *Screen* vol. 43 no. 1, Spring 2002, pp. 41–56.

3 The performance of celebrity is discussed in Chapter 3.

4 James Naremore, *Acting in the Cinema* (Berkeley: University of California
Press, 1988), p. 3.

5 See Sharon Marie Carnicke, 'Screen Performance and Directors'
Visions', in Cynthia Baron, Diane Carson and Frank P. Tomasulo (eds),

More Than a Method: Trends and Traditions in Contemporary Screen Performance (Detroit, MI: Wayne State University Press, 2004). Also Sharon Marie Carnicke, 'The Material Poetry of Acting: "Objects of Attention", Performance Style, and Gender in *The Shining* and *Eyes Wide Shut*', *Journal of Film and Video* vol. 58 nos 1–2, Spring/Summer 2006, pp. 21–30.

6   See Naremore, *Acting in the Cinema*, p. 3. Also Drake, 'Reconceptualizing Screen Performance', p. 86.

7   See Drake, 'Reconceptualizing Screen Performance', p. 85.

8   See, for example, the comments in response to David Thomson, 'Nicole Kidman Is Queen of the Flops', *Guardian*, 8 December 2008. Available online: <http://www.guardian.co.uk/film/filmblog/2008/dec/08/nicole-kidman-angelina-jolie?commentpage=1>. Accessed 22 March 2011.

9   See Willa Paskin and Claude Brodesser-Akner, 'The Star Market: Can *Rabbit Hole* Help Nicole Kidman Reconnect with Audiences?', *New York Magazine Vulture Section*, 24 December 2010. Available online: <http://nymag.com/daily/entertainment/2010/12/nicole_kidman_star_market.html>. Accessed 18 March 2011. Also Rohin Guha, 'Why Does America Have Trust Issues with Female Celebrities?', *BlackBook*, 27 January 2010. Available online: <http://www.blackbookmag.com/article/why-does-america-have-trust-issues-with-female-celebrities/15505>. Accessed 25 May 2011.

10   See Graham F. Thompson, 'Approaches to "Performance": An Analysis of Terms', *Screen* vol. 26 no. 5, 1985, p. 85.

11   See John O'Donnell, 'Nicole Kidman: Flaming Star', *Rolling Stone* (Australia) no. 432, June 1989, p. 42.

12   See Brian McFarlane, 'Phil Noyce: *Dead Calm*', *Cinema Papers* no. 73, May 1989, p. 8.

13   See sound interview, 'Phillip Noyce in Conversation with Andrew Urban', *Metro Screen* Recorded Events, 3 March 2009, 30'–33'. Available online: <http://metroscreen.org.au/_blog/Recorded_Events/post/Phillip_Noyce_in_Conversation_with_Andrew_Urban/>. Accessed 24 March 2011.

14   O'Donnell, 'Nicole Kidman', p. 42.

15   McFarlane, 'Phil Noyce', p. 11.

16   Naremore, *Acting in the Cinema*, discusses these distinctions, pp. 34–45.

17   See discussion in Pam Cook, *Baz Luhrmann* (London: BFI, 2010), p. 78.

18   See Tom O'Regan, *Australian National Cinema* (London and New York: Routledge, 1996), pp. 106–10.

19   See Naremore, *Acting in the Cinema*, pp. 281–2.

20   See, for example, Dave Kehr, 'Thriller "Dead Calm" Has the Skill But Not the Soul', *Chicago Tribune*, 7 April 1989. Available online: <http://articles.chicagotribune.com/1989-04-07/entertainment/8904020190_1_orson-welles-calm-orpheus/2>. Accessed 25 March 2011.

21   See Chapter 1.

22   See Bernard Weinraub, 'How "To Die For" Managed to Open at Simpson Finale', *New York Times*, 10 October 1995. Available online: <http://www.nytimes.com/1995/10/10/movies/how-to-die-for-managed-to-open-at-simpson-finale.html?ref=gusvansant&pagewanted=1>. Accessed 29 March 2011.

23   See Peter Travers, '*To Die For*', *Rolling Stone*, 6 October 1995. Available online: <http://www.rollingstone.com/movies/reviews/to-die-for-19950101>. Accessed 29 March 2011.

24   Drake, 'Reconceptualizing Screen Performance', pp. 86–7. See also Thompson's discussion in 'Approaches to "Performance"', pp. 78–90. And Carnicke, 'The Material Poetry of Acting', p. 29.

25   For example, Leslie Bennetts, 'La Femme Nicole', *Vanity Fair*, July 1995, p. 128. Also Ingrid Sischy, 'Nicole's New Light', *Vanity Fair* no. 508, December 2002, p. 245.

26   See Bob Strauss, 'A Role to Die For', *Los Angeles Daily News*, 5 October 1995. Available online: <http://articles.sun-sentinel.com/1995-10-05/lifestyle/9510040328_1_suzanne-stone-nicole-kidman-drugstore-cowboy>. Accessed 30 March 2011. Also David Thomson, *Nicole Kidman* (London: Bloomsbury, 2006), p. 75.

27 Benjamin Svetkey, 'Seeing Red', *Entertainment Weekly* no. 278, 9 June 1995. Available online: <http://www.ew.com/ew/article/0,,297523,00.html>. Accessed 29 March 2011.

28 See Thomson, *Nicole Kidman*, p. 82.

29 Martin Shingler makes similar points about Bette Davis's acting, including the use of her voice, in 'Bette Davis: Malevolence in Motion', in Alan Lovell and Peter Krämer (eds), *Screen Acting* (London and New York: Routledge, 1999), pp. 52–3.

30 Kidman imitated Marilyn Monroe's voice for the part of Norman Jean in Kennedy Miller's *Happy Feet* (2006).

31 IMDb has a full list of awards for *To Die For*. <http://www.imdb.com/title/tt0114681/awards>. Accessed 31 March 2011.

32 See Dennis Bingham, 'Kidman, Cruise, and Kubrick: A Brechtian Pastiche', in Baron, Carson and Tomasulo (eds), *More Than a Method*, p. 249.

33 See, for example, Thomson, *Nicole Kidman*, pp. 103–18.

34 See Michael Shnayerson, 'Portrait of an Actress: Nicole Kidman's Remarkable Year', *Vanity Fair* no. 446, October 1997, pp. 198, 225–7.

35 See Tom Junod, 'A Bridge, a Bed, a Bar and a Real Ozzie Gull: The Days and Nights Nicole Kidman Spent with Tom … Junod', *Esquire* vol. 132 no. 2, 1 August 1999, pp. 5, 68–75, 142. Available online: <http://www.esquire.com/women/nicole-kidman-gallery-0899>. Accessed 6 April 2011.

36 See Nancy Collins, 'Lust and Trust', *Rolling Stone*, 8 July 1999. Also appears in *Rolling Stone* (Australia) no. 565, September 1999, pp. 44–50, 110.

37 See Thomson, *Nicole Kidman*, p. 109.

38 See Carnicke, 'Screen Performance and Directors' Visions', pp. 59–61. Also Carnicke, 'The Material Poetry of Acting', pp. 24–5.

39 See Bingham, 'Kidman, Cruise, and Kubrick', p. 250.

40 See James Naremore, *On Kubrick* (London: BFI, 2007), pp. 231–7.

41 See Bingham, 'Kidman, Cruise, and Kubrick', pp. 253–9.

42 Bingham, 'Kidman, Cruise, and Kubrick', p. 259.

43 For example, David Denby, '*Eyes Wide Shut*', *New Yorker*, 2 August 1999. Available online: <http://www.newyorker.com/arts/reviews/film/eyes_wide_shut_kubrick>; Andrew Sarris, 'Eyes Don't Have It: Kubrick's Turgid Finale', *New York Observer*, 25 July 1999. Available online: <http://www.observer.com/node/41785>; J. Hoberman, 'I Wake Up Dreaming', *Village Voice*, 20 July 1999. Available online: <http://www.villagevoice.com/1999-07-20/film/i-wake-up-dreaming/>, accessed 5 April 2011.

44 See Carnicke, 'Screen Performance and Directors' Visions', pp. 60–1.

45 *Eyes Wide Shut* performed badly at the box office and received mixed reviews on its initial release. Among its meagre award nominations, Kidman received two for her performance, one of which she won. See IMDb: <http://www.imdb.com/title/tt0120663/awards>. Accessed 15 April 2011.

46 See, for example, Michael Wood, 'Quite a Night', *London Review of Books* vol. 21 no. 19, 30 September 1999, pp. 51–3.

47 Thompson discusses approaches to reading character in 'Approaches to "Performance"', pp. 88–90.

48 See Randy A. Nelson *et al.*, 'What's an Oscar Worth?', *Economic Enquiry* vol. 39 no. 1, January 2001, pp. 1–16.

49 See Sukhdev Sandhu, 'Masterpiece of Miscasting', *Telegraph*, 14 February 2003. Available online: <http://www.telegraph.co.uk/culture/film/3589841/Masterpiece-of-miscasting.html>. Accessed 21 April 2011.

50 See Paramount Pictures' *The Hours* production notes. Available online: <http://www.cinema.com/articles/1654/hours-the-production-notes.phtml>. Accessed 27 April 2011.

51 See John Hiscock, 'Nicole Kidman as Never Seen Before', *Telegraph*, 2 November 2002. Available online: <http://www.telegraph.co.uk/culture/film/3585117/Nicole-Kidman-as-never-seen-before.html>. Accessed 28 April 2011.

52 See Michael Cunningham, 'Nicole Kidman', *Interview*, February 2002, pp. 92–101.

53 Woolf's recorded voice can be heard at: <http://news.bbc.co.uk/1/hi/ 7684225.stm>. Accessed 28 April 2011.

54 For example, Hiscock, "Nicole Kidman As Never Seen Before'; Rob Blackwelder, 'Half an Hour about "The Hours"', *SPLICEDwire* 2002, n.d. Available online: <http://www.splicedwire.com/02features/ cunninghamhare.html>. Accessed 28 April 2011; Alona Wartofsky, 'Kidman Stares Down the Woolf in "The Hours"', *Washington Post*, 10 January 2003. Available online: <http://www.lawrence.com/news/ 2003/jan/10/kidman_stares/>. Accessed 28 April 2011; Stephen Holden, 'Who's Afraid Like Virginia Woolf?', *New York Times*, 27 December 2002. Available online: <http://movies.nytimes.com/movie/review?res= 9C0DE6DE113CF934A15751C1A9649C8B63>. Accessed 28 April 2011; Dennis Lim, 'Dances with Woolf', *Village Voice*, 24 December 2002. Available online: <http://www.villagevoice.com/2002-12-24/film/ dances-with-woolf/1/>. Accessed 28 April 2011.

55 Kevin Esch, '"I Don't See Any Method at All": The Problem of Actorly Transformation', *Journal of Film and Video* vol. 58 nos 1–2, Spring/ Summer 2006, pp. 98–9.

56 Esch, '"I Don't See Any Method at All"', p. 105. Esch uses Robert De Niro as an example of quintessential actorly transformation in his approach to his roles.

57 See IMDb awards history for *The Hours*: <http://www.imdb.com/title/ tt0274558/awards>. Accessed 2 May 2011.

58 See A. O. Scott, 'A Unified Theory of Nicole Kidman', *New York Times*, 2 November 2003. Available online: <http://www.nytimes.com/ 2003/11/02/movies/a-unified-theory-of-nicole-kidman.html>. Accessed 2 May 2011.

59 See Wendy Parkins, '"Whose Face Was It?": Nicole Kidman, Virginia Woolf, and the Boundaries of Feminine Celebrity', in Anna Burrells *et al.* (eds), *Woolfian Boundaries: Selected Papers from the Sixteenth Annual Conference on Virginia Woolf* (Bakersfield: California State University, 2007), pp. 144–9. Available online: <http://www.csub.edu/woolf_center/ publication16/pdf/vw_publication16_fullbook.pdf>.

60 See Megan Baker, 'Complex and Contradictory: The Enduring Stardom of Virginia Woolf', *Journal of Undergraduate Research* vol. 1 no. 5, 2008–9, pp. 1–30. Available online: <http://www.nd.edu/~ujournal/archive/08-09/print/>. Accessed 4 May 2011.

61 Bingham, 'Kidman, Cruise, and Kubrick', pp. 259–60.

62 See Cook, *Baz Luhrmann*, p. 78.

63 Philip Auslander, 'Postmodernism and Performance', in Steven Connor (ed.), *The Cambridge Companion to Postmodernism* (Cambridge: Cambridge University Press, 2004), pp. 103–4.

64 Auslander, 'Postmodernism and Performance', p. 106.

65 Helen Gilbert and Joanne Tompkins, *Post-colonial Drama: Theory, Practice, Politics* (Oxford and New York: Routledge, 1996), p. 3. See also Joseph R. Roach, 'Postcolonial Studies', in Janelle G. Reinelt and Joseph R. Roach (eds), *Critical Theory and Performance* (Ann Arbor: University of Michigan Press, 2007).

66 See Joanne Tompkins, 'Performing History's Unsettlement', in Reinelt and Roach, *Critical Theory and Performance*, pp. 71–3.

67 For example, Mick LaSalle, 'Movie Review: One Fair Lady Meets Aussie Cowboy', *San Francisco Chronicle*, 26 November 2008. Available online: <http://articles.sfgate.com/2008-11-26/entertainment/17127043_1_baz-luhrmann-nicole-kidman-aborigine>. Accessed 10 May 2011. Glenn Milne, 'Film Director Baz Luhrmann Blasts Nicole Kidman Critics', *Courier-Mail* (Brisbane), 24 January 2009.

68 See Manohla Dargis, 'Oh Give Me a Home Where the Cowboys and Kangaroos Roam', *New York Times*, 26 November 2008. Available online: <http://movies.nytimes.com/2008/11/26/movies/26aust.html>. Accessed 10 May 2011. Matt Mueller, '*Australia*', *Total Film*, 14 January 2009. Available online: <http://www.mattmueller.co.uk/index.php?page_id=Reviews&category_id=Cinema&article_id=136>. Accessed 10 May 2011.

69 See Roach, 'Postcolonial Studies', p. 68.

70 Kidman's whiteness is discussed in Chapter 3. See pp. 104–8.

71 Carnicke, 'Screen Performance and Directors' Visions', p. 49.

72 See Pamela Robertson Wojcik, 'The Sound of Film Acting', *Journal of Film and Video* vol. 58 nos 1–2, Spring/Summer 2006, pp. 71–2.

73 See Philip Auslander, *From Acting to Performance: Essays in Modernism and Postmodernism* (New York and London: Routledge, 1997).

74 See Wojcik, 'The Sound of Film Acting', pp. 80–1.

75 Bingham, 'Kidman, Cruise, and Kubrick', p. 260.

76 See illustrations in Naremore, *Acting in the Cinema*, pp. 54–9.

77 Paul Wells discusses issues of live-action and animated stardom in 'To Affinity and Beyond: Woody, Buzz and the New Authenticity', in Thomas Austin and Martin Barker (eds), *Contemporary Hollywood Stardom* (London: Arnold, 2003).

3 Persona

1 Barry King, 'Stardom, Celebrity, and the Money Form', *Velvet Light Trap* vol. 65, Spring 2010, pp. 7–19.

2 King, 'Stardom, Celebrity, and the Money Form', p. 9.

3 For example King, 'Stardom, Celebrity, and the Money Form'.

4 King, 'Stardom, Celebrity, and the Money Form', p. 9.

5 Philip Drake, 'Who Owns Celebrity?: Privacy, Publicity and the Legal Regulation of Celebrity Images', in Sean Redmond and Su Holmes (eds), *Stardom and Celebrity: A Reader* (London: Sage, 2007), p. 228.

6 See Stephen M. Silverman, 'Kidman Has Law on Her Side in Libel Case', *People*, 14 October 2003. Available online: <http://www.people.com/people/article/0,,627106,00.html>. Accessed 18 May 2011.

7 See 'Kidman Wins Affair Libel Case', *CNN Entertainment*, 31 July 2003. Available online: <http://articles.cnn.com/2003-07-31/entertainment/uk.kidman.mail_1_libel-paul-dacre-substantial-undisclosed-damages?_s=PM:SHOWBIZ>. Accessed 18 May 2011.

8 See Christopher Bagley, 'Nicole: Nicole Kidman Turns Dark Days into a Dazzling Career', *W* vol. 32 no. 12, December 2003.

9   Drake, 'Who Owns Celebrity?', p. 226. At the time of writing, UK privacy laws and media rights are under review following the 2011 News International phone-hacking scandal.

10 See, for example, 'Another Kid for Kidman? Nicole Reveals Glimpse of Bump Sparking Baby Rumours', *Daily Mail*, 18 June 2010. Available online: <http://www.dailymail.co.uk/tvshowbiz/article-1287420/Nicole-Kidman-reveals-glimpse-bump-sparking-baby-rumours.html>. Accessed 19 May 2011.

11 See Eleanor Young, 'Could Baby Number Two Be on the Way for Nicole Kidman?', *Marie Claire*, 24 November 2009. Available online: <http://www.marieclaire.co.uk/news/celebrity/432061/could-baby-number-two-be-on-the-way-for-nicole-kidman.html>. Accessed 19 May 2011.

12 P. David Marshall, *Celebrity and Power: Fame in Contemporary Culture* (Minneapolis: University of Minnesota Press, 1997), p. 121.

13 Marshall, *Celebrity and Power*, pp. 125–6.

14 David Thomson, *Nicole Kidman* (London: Bloomsbury, 2006), pp. 234–6.

15 The teaser can be viewed on YouTube: <http://www.youtube.com/watch?v=ZENjHwlrG98>. Accessed 20 May 2011.

16 Interview available on YouTube: <http://www.youtube.com/watch?v=77hX09_DFUM> and <http://www.youtube.com/watch?v=KlsLZ7JLhUQ>. Accessed 20 May 2011.

17 See Chapter 1, pp. 22, 29.

18 For example, *Vanity Fair* no. 566, October 2007, has a cover image of Kidman, looking into camera with lips parted, sporting a sailor's cap and exposing her upper torso to the waist to reveal her plunge bra. The byline reads 'Nicole Kidman bares all'.

19 Thomson, *Nicole Kidman*, p. 240.

20 See Sally Singer, 'Master Class', *Vogue*, September 2003, pp. 642–62.

21 *Vogue*, September 2003, p. 84.

22 Singer, 'Master Class', p. 658.

23 Singer, 'Master Class', p. 644.

24 See this chapter, pp. 76–8.

25 For example, Carol Driver, 'Nicole Kidman's Fitness Regime to Lose
    Baby Curves for Next Film Role – Playing a Transsexual', *Daily Mail*,
    30 November 2009. Available online: <http://www.dailymail.co.uk/
    tvshowbiz/article-1232055/Nicole-Kidmans-fitness-regime-lose-baby-
    curves-latest-film-role—playing-transsexual.html>. Accessed 25 May
    2011.

26 See Rachael Jones, 'Is Nicole Kidman Expecting?', *Age*, 9 June 2010.
    Available online: <http://media.theage.com.au/entertainment/red-carpet/
    is-nicole-kidman-expecting-1580822.html>. Accessed 25 May 2011.

27 See 'Another Kid for Kidman?'.

28 See 'Nicole Kidman Denies Pregnancy Rumours', *Yummy Life & Style*,
    4 December 2010. Available online: <http://yummylifestyle.com/
    2010/12/nicole-kidman-denies-pregnancy-rumours1242010009>.
    Accessed 25 May 2011.

29 See 'Kidman, Urban Have 2nd Child through Surrogate', *Washington
    Times*, 18 January 2011. Available online: <http://www.washingtontimes.
    com/news/2011/jan/18/kidman-urban-have-2nd-child-through-
    surrogate/>. Accessed 25 May 2011.

30 See Erica Hurtz, 'Nine Plastic Surgery Procedures that Nicole Kidman
    Had', *Make {Me} Heal*, 21 December 2009. Available online:
    <http://news.makemeheal.com/celebrity-plastic-surgery/nicole-kidman-
    nine-plastic-surgery-2>. Accessed 26 May 2011.

31 For some actors, plastic surgery can lead to professional suicide, as in the
    case of Mickey Rourke.

32 See Willa Paskin, 'Nicole Kidman's Forehead Is Back!: An Animated
    Retrospective', *New York Magazine Vulture Section*, 15 December 2010.
    Available online: <http://nymag.com/daily/entertainment/2010/12/
    we_warmly_welcome_back_nicole.html>. Accessed 26 May 2011.

33 See Grayson Cooke, 'Effacing the Face: Botox and the Anarchivic
    Archive', *Body & Society* vol. 14 no. 2, 2008, pp. 25–7.

34 See Charlotte Triggs with Maureen Harrington, 'Botox Confessions',
    People vol. 70 no. 21, 24 November 2008. Available online:

<http://www.people.com/people/archive/article/0,,20245470,00.html>.
Accessed 26 May 2011.

35 See Amelia Hill, 'Actors Warned to Keep off the Botox', *Observer*,
9 February 2003. Available online: <http://www.guardian.co.uk/uk/
2003/feb/09/film.filmnews>. Accessed 26 May 2011.

36 See 'Kidman Admits to Botox Face Freeze', *Herald Sun*, 13 January
2011. Available online: <http://www.heraldsun.com.au/ipad/kidman-
admits-to-botox-face-freeze/story-fn6bn80a-1225986555083>.
Accessed 26 May 2011.

37 See Laura M. Holson, 'A Little Too Ready for Her Close-up?', *New York
Times*, 23 April 2010. Available online: <http://www.nytimes.com/
2010/04/25/fashion/25natural.html?ref=style&pagewanted=all>.
Accessed 26 May 2011.

38 See 'Back to the Botox? Nicole Kidman Displays Suspiciously Frozen
Features at the CMAs', *Daily Mail*, 4 April 2011. Available online:
<http://www.dailymail.co.uk/tvshowbiz/article-1373123/ACM-Awards-
Nicole-Kidman-displays-suspiciously-frozen-features.html>. Accessed
26 May 2011.

39 See discussion in Cooke, 'Effacing the Face', pp. 23–38.

40 See Paul McDonald, 'Stars in the Online Universe: Promotion, Nudity,
Reverence', in Thomas Austin and Martin Barker (eds), *Contemporary
Hollywood Stardom* (London: Edward Arnold, 2003), p. 32.

41 See <http://www.nkidman.com>. Accessed 13 June 2011.

42 McDonald, 'Stars in the Online Universe', pp. 40–2.

43 See Justin Wyatt, 'Uncertainty in the Marketplace: The Development of
the Contemporary Industry Structure', in *High Concept: Movies and
Marketing in Hollywood* (Austin: University of Texas Press, 1994),
pp. 81–93.

44 Kidman's commercials for these brands can be seen on YouTube.

45 See IMDb News for Baz Luhrmann: <http://www.imdb.com/name/
nm0525303/news?year=2004>. Accessed 30 May 2011.

46 Thomson, *Nicole Kidman*, p. 244, refers to *No. 5 The Film* as a
'movielette'.

47 For example: Martin Scorsese's *Bleu de Chanel* (2010) with Gaspard Ulliel; Sofia Coppola's *Miss Dior Chérie* (2011) with Natalie Portman; Frank Miller's *Gucci Guilty* (2010) with Evan Rachel Wood.

48 See Pam Cook, *Baz Luhrmann* (London: BFI, 2010), pp. 32–3, 110–15.

49 Paul Grainge discusses the branding operations in *No. 5 The Film* in *Brand Hollywood: Selling Entertainment in a Global Media Age* (Oxford and New York: Routledge, 2008), pp. 38–42.

50 See *Look to the Stars: The World of Celebrity Giving:* <http://www. looktothestars.org/celebrity/185-nicole-kidman>. Accessed 31 May 2011.

51 Transcript available online: <http://www.unifem.org/news_events/ story_detail.php?StoryID=957>. Accessed 31 May 2011.

52 See *It's an Honour* website: <http://www.itsanhonour.gov.au/honours/ honour_roll/search.cfm?aus_award_id=1131287&search_type=simple& showInd=true>. Accessed 31 May 2011.

53 Transcript available online: <http://www.unifem.org/news_events/ story_detail.php?StoryID=1008>. Accessed 31 May 2011.

54 See *UsMagazine*: <http://www.usmagazine.com/celebritynews/ news/nicole-kidman-brad-paisley-raise-17-million-for-nashville-flood-relief-2010175>. Accessed 31 May 2011.

55 See Janet Street-Porter, 'Nicole's Sex Roles Betray Women in the Real World', *Independent*, 25 October 2009. Available online: <http://www.independent.co.uk/opinion/columnists/janet-street-porter/editoratlarge-nicoles-sex-roles—betray-women-in-the-real-world-1808989.html>. Accessed 31 May 2011.

56 See Samantha Morton, 'Why Nicole Kidman Was Brave to Speak Out', *Guardian*, 26 October 2009. Available online: <http://www.guardian. co.uk/film/2009/oct/26/nicole-kidman>. Accessed 31 May 2011.

57 For example Grainge, *Brand Hollywood*, pp. 5–6.

58 See Tom Junod, 'A Bridge, a Bed, a Bar, and a Real Ozzie Gull', *Esquire*, 1 August 1999. Available online: <http://www.esquire.com/women/ women-we-love/nicole-kidman-gallery-0899>. Accessed 7 June 2011.

59 See David Murray, 'Nicole Kidman Will Not Live in Sydney', *Sunday Telegraph*, 13 December 2009. Available online: <http://www.

dailytelegraph.com.au/news/nicole-will-not-live-in-sydney/story-e6frewt0-1225809770647>. Accessed 7 June 2011.

60 The links between US and Australian colonial history are discussed by Holly Randell-Moon in her editorial introduction to the Post-racial States issue of *Critical Race and Whiteness Studies* vol. 7 no. 1, 2011, pp. 6–7. Available online: <http://acrawsa.org.au/ejournal/?id=51>. Accessed 8 June 2011.

61 Kidman was born in Hawaii and lived for a while in Washington, DC before moving to Sydney, Australia when she was four years old.

62 Thomson, *Nicole Kidman*, pp. 18–25, has a chapter on Kidman's Australian background.

63 See Liz Conor, *The Spectacular Modern Woman: Feminine Visibility in the 1920s* (Bloomington: Indiana University Press, 2004), p. 3.

64 Conor, *The Spectacular Modern Woman*, p. xv.

65 Conor, *The Spectacular Modern Woman*, pp. 9–10.

66 Conor, *The Spectacular Modern Woman*, p. 132.

67 Conor, *The Spectacular Modern Woman*, p. 186.

68 Conor, *The Spectacular Modern Woman*, p. 169.

69 Conor, *The Spectacular Modern Woman*, p. xv.

70 For example, Ruth Frankenberg (ed.), *Displacing Whiteness: Essays in Social and Cultural Criticism* (Durham, NC: Duke University Press, 1997), pp. 1–34; Richard Dyer, 'The Matter of Whiteness', in *White* (London and New York: Routledge, 1997).

71 Dyer, *White*, p. 21.

72 Dyer, *White*, p. 23.

73 Dyer, *White*, p. 30.

74 Conor, *The Spectacular Modern Woman*, p. 168.

75 See *Vanity Fair* no. 566, October 2007, p. 19.

76 See Gwendolyn Audrey Foster, *Performing Whiteness: Postmodern Re/Constructions in the Cinema* (New York: SUNY Press, 2003).

77 Dyer, *White*, p. 4.

78 See Debbie Kruger, 'The Art of Growing Up as an Actress', *Australian*, 1 December 1986. Available online: <http://www.debbiekruger.com/

writer/freelance/nic.html>. Accessed 7 June 2011; Junod, 'A Bridge, a Bed, a Bar, and a Real Ozzie Gull'; 'Nicole Kidman's Flawless White Moment', *refinery29.com*, 29 October 2010. Available online: <http://www.refinery29.com/nicole-kidman-looks-flawless-on-the-red-carpet>. Accessed 7 June 2011.

79 See Sherryl Vint, 'The New Backlash: Popular Culture's "Marriage" with Feminism, or Love Is All You Need', *Journal of Popular Film and Television* vol. 34 no. 4, 2007, pp. 160–9.

80 Vint, 'The New Backlash', pp. 167–8.

81 See Tom O'Regan, *Australian National Cinema* (London and New York: Routledge, 1996), pp. 172, 288–303.

82 See Andrew Gans, 'James Franco Says He Will Join Nicole Kidman for Broadway Revival of *Sweet Bird of Youth*', *Playbill.com*, 31 January 2011. Available online: http://www.playbill.com/news/article/147187-James-Franco-Says-He-Will-Join-Nicole-Kidman-for-Broadway-Revival-of-Sweet-Bird-of-Youth>. Accessed 19 July 2011.

BIBLIOGRAPHY

The bibliography lists books and articles cited in the text. Online, press and other resources are dealt with in chapter endnotes.

Auslander, Philip, *From Acting to Performance: Essays in Modernism and Postmodernism* (New York and London: Routledge, 1997).

Auslander, Philip, 'Postmodernism and Performance', in Steven Connor (ed.), *The Cambridge Companion to Postmodernism* (Cambridge: Cambridge University Press, 2004).

Austin, Thomas and Barker, Martin (eds), *Contemporary Hollywood Stardom* (London: Edward Arnold, 2003).

Baker, Megan, 'Complex and Contradictory: The Enduring Stardom of Virginia Woolf', *Journal of Undergraduate Research* vol. 1 no. 5, 2008–9.

Baron, Cynthia, Carson, Diane and Tomasulo, Frank P. (eds), *More Than a Method: Trends and Traditions in Contemporary Film Performance* (Detroit, MI: Wayne State University Press, 2004).

Bingham, Dennis, 'Kidman, Cruise, and Kubrick: A Brechtian Pastiche', in Baron, Carson and Tomasulo (eds), *More Than a Method*.

Carnicke, Sharon Marie, 'Screen Performance and Directors' Visions', in Baron, Carson and Tomasulo (eds), *More Than a Method*.

Carnicke, Sharon Marie, 'The Material Poetry of Acting: "Objects of Attention", Performance Style, and Gender in *The Shining* and *Eyes Wide Shut*', *Journal of Film and Video* vol. 58 nos 1–2, Spring/Summer 2006.

Conor, Liz, 'Nicole Kidman and the Commodity Star', *Metro* vol. 127 no. 8, April 2001.

Conor, Liz, *The Spectacular Modern Woman: Feminine Visibility in the 1920s* (Bloomington: Indiana University Press, 2004).

Cook, Pam, *Baz Luhrmann* (London: BFI, 2010).

Cooke, Grayson, 'Effacing the Face: Botox and the Anarchivic Archive', *Body & Soul* vol. 14 no. 2, 2008.

DeCordova, Richard, *Picture Personalities: The Emergence of the Star System in America* (Champaign: University of Illinois Press, 2001).

Delamoir, Jeannette, 'Eyes Wide Shut: Tom, Nicole, Stardom and Visual Memory', *Transformations* vol. 3, June 2002.

Drake, Philip, 'Reconceptualizing Screen Performance', *Journal of Film and Video* vol. 58 nos 1–2, Spring/Summer 2006.

Drake, Philip, 'Who Owns Celebrity?: Privacy, Publicity and the Legal Regulation of Celebrity Images', in Redmond and Holmes (eds), *Stardom and Celebrity*.

Dyer, Richard, *White* (New York and London: Routledge, 1997).

Dyer, Richard, *Stars* (London: BFI, 1998).

Dyer, Richard, *Heavenly Bodies: Film Stars and Society* (London and New York: Routledge, 2004).

Ellis, John, 'Stars as a Cinematic Phenomenon', in *Visible Fictions: Cinema, Television, Video* (London and New York: Routledge, 1992).

Esch, Kevin, '"I Don't See Any Method at All": The Problem of Actorly Transformation', *Journal of Film and Video* vol. 58 nos 1–2, Spring/Summer 2006.

Foster, Gwendolyn Audrey, *Performing Whiteness: Postmodern Re/Constructions in the Cinema* (New York: SUNY Press, 2003).

Frankenberg, Ruth (ed.), *Displacing Whiteness: Essays in Social and Cultural Criticism* (Durham, NC: Duke University Press, 1997).

Gamson, Joshua, *Claims to Fame: Celebrity in Modern America* (Berkeley: University of California Press, 1994).

Geraghty, Christine, 'Re-examining Stardom: Questions of Texts, Bodies and Performance', in Christine Gledhill and Linda Williams (eds), *Reinventing Film Studies* (London: Arnold, 2000).

Geraghty, Christine, 'Crossing Over: Performing as a Lady and a Dame', *Screen* vol. 43 no. 1, Spring 2002.

Gilbert, Helen and Tompkins, Joanne, *Post-colonial Drama: Theory, Practice, Politics* (Oxford and New York: Routledge, 1996).

Grainge, Paul, *Brand Hollywood: Selling Entertainment in a Global Media Age* (Oxford and New York: Routledge, 2008).

King, Barry, 'Stardom, Celebrity, and the Money Form', *Velvet Light Trap* vol. 65, Spring 2010.

Kubrick, Stanley and Raphael, Frederic, *Eyes Wide Shut: A Screenplay by Stanley Kubrick and Frederic Raphael* (Harmondsworth: Penguin, 1999).

Marshall, P. David, *Celebrity and Power: Fame in Contemporary Culture* (Minneapolis: University of Minnesota Press, 1997).

McDonald, Paul, *The Star System: Hollywood's Production of Popular Identities* (London: Wallflower Press, 2000).

McDonald, Paul, 'Stars in the Online Universe: Promotion, Nudity, Reverence', in Austin and Barker (eds), *Contemporary Hollywood Stardom*.

McFarlane, Brian, 'Phil Noyce: *Dead Calm*', *Cinema Papers* no. 73, May 1989.

Naremore, James, *Acting in the Cinema* (Berkeley: University of California Press, 1988).

Naremore, James, *On Kubrick* (London: BFI, 2007).

Nelson, Randy A. *et al.*, 'What's an Oscar Worth?', *Economic Enquiry* vol. 39 no. 1, January 2001.

O'Regan, Tom, *Australian National Cinema* (London and New York: Routledge, 1996).

Parkins, Wendy, '"Whose Face Was It?": Nicole Kidman, Virginia Woolf, and the Boundaries of Feminine Celebrity', in Anna Burrells *et al.* (eds), *Woolfian Boundaries: Selected Papers from the Sixteenth Annual Conference on Virginia Woolf* (Bakersfield: California State University, 2007).

Randell-Moon, Holly, 'Editorial', *Critical Race and Whiteness Studies* vol. 7 no. 1, 2011.

Rayner, Jonathan, *Contemporary Australian Cinema: An Introduction* (Manchester: Manchester University Press, 2000).

Redmond, Sean and Holmes, Su (eds), *Stardom and Celebrity: A Reader* (London: Sage, 2007).

Reinelt, Janelle G. and Roach, Joseph R. (eds), *Critical Theory and Performance* (Ann Arbor: University of Michigan Press, 2007).

Roach, Joseph R., 'Postcolonial Studies', in Reinelt and Roach (eds), *Critical Theory and Performance*.

Shingler, Martin, 'Bette Davis: Malevolence in Motion', in Alan Lovell and Peter Krämer (eds), *Screen Acting* (London and New York: Routledge, 1999).

Thompson, Graham F., 'Approaches to "Performance": An Analysis of Terms', *Screen* vol. 26 no. 5, 1985.

Thomson, David, *Nicole Kidman* (London: Bloomsbury, 2006).

Tompkins, Joanne, 'Performing History's Unsettlement', in Reinelt and Roach (eds), *Critical Theory and Performance*.

Vint, Sherryl, 'The New Backlash: Popular Culture's "Marriage" with Feminism, or Love Is All You Need', *Journal of Popular Film and Television* vol. 34 no. 4, 2007.

Wells, Paul, 'To Affinity and Beyond: Woody, Buzz and the New Authenticity', in Austin and Barker (eds), *Contemporary Hollywood Stardom*.

Wojcik, Pamela Robertson, 'The Sound of Film Acting', *Journal of Film and Video* vol. 58 nos 1–2, Spring/Summer 2006.

Wyatt, Justin, 'Uncertainty in the Marketplace: The Development of the Contemporary Industry Structure', in *High Concept: Movies and Marketing in Hollywood* (Austin: University of Texas Press, 1994).

Wyatt, Justin, 'The Formation of the "Major Independent": Miramax, New Line and the New Hollywood', in Steve Neale and Murray Smith (eds), *Contemporary Hollywood Cinema* (London and New York: Routledge, 1998).

FILMOGRAPHY (in date order)

Feature films and television

CHASE THROUGH THE NIGHT (Howard Rubie, Australia, 1983) [television movie] Petra.

SKIN DEEP (Mark Joffe, Chris Langman, Australia, 1983) [television movie] Sheena Henderson.

BUSH CHRISTMAS (Henri Safran, Australia, 1983) Helen.

BMX BANDITS (Brian Trenchard-Smith, Australia, 1983) Judy.

MATTHEW AND SON (Gary Conway, Australia, 1984) [television movie] Bridget Elliot.

A COUNTRY PRACTICE: REPAIRING THE DAMAGE (Australia, Gary Conway, 1984) [television series] Simone Jenkins (2 episodes).

WINNERS: ROOM TO MOVE (John Duigan, Australia, 1985) [television series] Carol Trig (1 episode).

FIVE MILE CREEK (Kevin James Dobson, Australia, 1985) [television series] Annie (12 episodes).

WILLS & BURKE (Bob Weis, Australia, 1985) Julia Matthews.

ARCHER (Denny Lawrence, Australia, 1985) [television movie] Catherine.

WINDRIDER (Vincent Monton, Australia, 1986) Jade.

THE BIT PART (Brendan Maher, Australia, 1987) Mary McAllister.

UN'AUSTRALIANA A ROMA (Sergio Martino, Italy, 1987) [television movie] Jill.

WATCH THE SHADOWS DANCE (*Nightmaster*, Mark Joffe, Australia/Canada, 1987) Amy Gabriel.

VIETNAM (John Duigan, Chris Noonan, Australia, 1987) [television mini-series] Megan Goddard.

EMERALD CITY (Michael Jenkins, Australia, 1988) Helen.

DEAD CALM (Phillip Noyce, Australia, 1989) Rae Ingram.

BANGKOK HILTON (Ken Cameron, Australia, 1989) [television mini-series] Katrina Stanton.

DAYS OF THUNDER (Tony Scott, USA, 1990) Dr Claire Lewicki.

FLIRTING (John Duigan, Australia, 1991) Nicola.

BILLY BATHGATE (Robert Benton, USA, 1991) Drew Preston.

FAR AND AWAY (Ron Howard, USA, 1992) Shannon Christie.

MALICE (Harold Becker, Canada/USA, 1993) Tracy Kennsinger.

MY LIFE (Bruce Joel Rubin, USA, 1993) Gail Jones.

TO DIE FOR (Gus Van Sant, UK/USA, 1995) Suzanne Stone Maretto.

BATMAN FOREVER (Joel Schumacher, USA/UK, 1995) Dr Chase Meridian.

THE PORTRAIT OF A LADY (Jane Campion, UK/USA, 1996) Isabel Archer.

THE LEADING MAN (John Duigan, UK, 1996) Academy Award presenter.

THE PEACEMAKER (Mimi Leder, USA, 1997) Dr Julia Kelly.

PRACTICAL MAGIC (Griffin Dunne, USA/Australia, 1998) Gillian Owens.

EYES WIDE SHUT (Stanley Kubrick, UK/USA, 1999) Alice Harford.

MOULIN ROUGE! (Baz Luhrmann, USA/Australia, 2001) Satine.

THE OTHERS (*Los otros*, Alejandro Amenábar, USA/Spain/France/Italy, 2001) Grace Stewart.

BIRTHDAY GIRL (Jez Butterworth, UK/USA, 2001) Sophia/Nadia.

PANIC ROOM (David Fincher, USA, 2002) Voice on telephone.

THE HOURS (Stephen Daldry, USA/UK, 2002) Virginia Woolf.

DOGVILLE (Lars von Trier, Denmark/Sweden/UK/France/Germany/Netherlands/Norway/Finland, 2003) Grace Margaret Mulligan.

THE HUMAN STAIN (Robert Benton, USA/Germany/France, 2003) Faunia Farley.

COLD MOUNTAIN (Anthony Minghella, USA/UK/Romania/Italy, 2003) Ada Monroe.

THE STEPFORD WIVES (Frank Oz, USA, 2004) Joanna Eberhart.

BIRTH (Jonathan Glazer, USA/Germany, 2004) Anna.

THE INTERPRETER (Sydney Pollack, UK/USA/France/Germany, 2005) Silvia Broome.

BEWITCHED (Nora Ephron, USA, 2005) Isabel Bigelow/Samantha.

FUR: AN IMAGINARY PORTRAIT OF DIANE ARBUS (Steven Shainberg, USA, 2006) Diane Arbus.

HAPPY FEET (George Miller, Australia/USA, 2006) Norma Jean (voice).

GOD GREW TIRED OF US: THE STORY OF LOST BOYS OF SUDAN (Christopher Dillon Quinn, Tommy Walker, USA, 2006) [television documentary] Narrator.

THE INVASION (Oliver Hirschbiegel, USA/Australia, 2007) Carol Bennell.

MARGOT AT THE WEDDING (Noah Baumbach, USA, 2007) Margot.

THE GOLDEN COMPASS (Chris Weitz, USA/UK, 2007) Marisa Coulter.

I HAVE NEVER FORGOTTEN YOU: THE LIFE AND LEGACY OF SIMON WIESENTHAL (Richard Trank, USA, 2007) [documentary] Narrator.

AUSTRALIA (Baz Luhrmann, Australia/USA/UK, 2008) Lady Sarah Ashley.

NINE (Rob Marshall, USA/Italy, 2009) Claudia.

RABBIT HOLE (John Cameron Mitchell, USA, 2010) Becca.

JUST GO WITH IT (Dennis Dugan, USA, 2011) Devlin Adams.

TRESPASS (Joel Schumacher, USA, 2011) Sarah.

HEMINGWAY & GELLHORN (Philip Kaufman, USA, 2012) [television movie] Martha Gellhorn.

THE PAPERBOY (Lee Daniels, USA, 2012) Charlotte Bless.

THE DANISH GIRL (n.d.) Einar Wegener/Lili Elbe.

As producer

IN THE CUT (Jane Campion, Australia/USA/UK, 2003)
RABBIT HOLE (2010)
MONTE CARLO (Thomas Bezucha, USA/Hungary, 2011)
THE DANISH GIRL (n.d.)

Music videos

'Bop Girl' (Gillian Armstrong, Australia, 1983) With Pat Wilson.
'Somethin' Stupid' (Vaughan Arnell, UK, 2001) With Robbie Williams.
'One Day I'll Fly Away' (Baz Luhrmann, Australia/USA, 2001) From *Moulin Rouge!*.

Commercials

EL CORTE INGLÉS (Alejandro Amenábar, 2002) Spanish department store.
NO. 5 THE FILM (Baz Luhrmann, 2004) Chanel No. 5 perfume.
NINTENDO DS BRAIN TRAINING (Paul Mignot, 2007) Computer game.
SCHWEPPES (Shekhar Kapur, 2009) Agrum' range of soft drinks.
OMEGA LADYMATIC (2011) Women's wristwatches.

Theatre

THE BLUE ROOM (Sam Mendes, 1998)

INDEX

Note: Page numbers in **bold** indicate detailed analysis; those in *italic* denote illustrations. *n* = endnote.

List of Illustrations

While considerable effort has been made to correctly identify the copyright holders, this has not been possible in all cases. We apologise for any apparent negligence and any omissions or corrections brought to our attention will be remedied in any future editions.

Eyes Wide Shut, © Warner Bros.; 'Somethin' Stupid', Vaughan Arnell, 2011, EMI Chrysalis; *Time* magazine cover (5 July 1999, vol. 154 no. 1), Time Warner; *BMX Bandits*, BMX Bandits/Nilsen Group of Companies; American *Vogue* portrait (January 1994), photograph: Rocky Schenck, Conde Nast Publications Ltd; *The Portrait of a Lady*, © PolyGram Film Productions B.V.; *Vanity Fair* portrait (December 2002), photograph: Mario Testino, Conde Nast Publications Ltd; *The Stepford Wives*, © Paramount Pictures/© DreamWorks LLC; *Rabbit Hole*, © Op Eve 2 LLC; *Dead Calm*, Kennedy Miller Productions Pty Ltd; *To Die For*, © Columbia Pictures Industries, Inc.; *The Hours*, © Miramax Film Corp./ © Paramount Pictures Corporation; *Moulin Rouge!*, © Twentieth Century-Fox Film Corporation; *Australia*, © Twentieth Century-Fox Film Corporation/ © Dune Entertainment III LLC; *The Ellen DeGeneres Show*, Time Telepictures Television/A Very Good Production Inc./Telepictures Productions; American *Vogue* portrait (September 2003), photograph: Annie Leibovitz, Conde Nast Publications Ltd; *Nicole's Magic* website, www.nkidman.com; *Chanel No. 5*, Bazfilm; *Bewitched*, © Columbia Pictures Industries, Inc.